Perfect Your
Tackle

•PERFECT YOUR•
TACKLE

John Bailey

The Crowood Press

First published in 1993 by
The Crowood Press Ltd
Ramsbury, Marlborough
Wiltshire SN8 2HR

British Library Cataloguing-in-Publication Data

A catalogue record for this book is available from
the British Library.

ISBN 1 85223 732 5

Photograph page 2: the author with a bream
taken at twenty yards on the float.

Photograph page 6: roach and centrepins
go together.

Designed by D & N Publishing
The Old Surgery
Crowle Road
Lambourn
Berkshire RG16 7NR

Imagesetting by FIDO Imagesetting, Witney,
Oxfordshire.

Printed and bound in Great Britain by BPCC
Hazell Books, Aylesbury.

Contents

Introduction

I don't think that any of us who were there will forget a particular evening in southern India. The camp was electric with excitement: Steve Harper had just landed a mahseer weighing an incredible 104lb. The battle had been heroic and we spectators were almost as exhausted as Steve himself. Apparently, this mahseer was the largest caught on rod and line for some 40 or 50 years. We were all, in short, euphoric. There was a lot of back-slapping and self-congratulation and Steve himself praised his tackle above all. He flexed the rod – 'This is what did the job' he said.

Steve's gillie that famous morning was the excellent Bhola. He simply smiled and said very little despite the lavish congratulations poured upon him. Steve pushed him a little bit further; 'Have you ever seen a bigger mahseer, Bhola?' he asked.

Bhola took his time and grinned. 'Well, sir, yes I have. A few years ago my mother caught one of 112lb! On a hand line! It took her over four hours to land it!' We all shut up after that.

Even very crude tackle can succeed, and the Indians certainly knew that expensive western rods and reels were not essential to success. But you could see their eyes light up when you presented them with an item of tackle from the west. There is a concept of enjoyment and though fish can be caught on a branch and a piece of twine, with a stick of dynamite or with a net, there is nothing to beat the thrill of playing a good fish on beau-

tiful tackle. Even those who fish to live realize this and for those of us who live to fish, tackle is all part of the luxurious sport that we love so much. For us, fishing is all about pleasure and we might as well get as much from the sport as possible. I do honestly believe that precise, delicate, superbly efficient tackle does actively increase our enjoyment of the fish we catch and even the very act of fishing. Just to see a beautifully balanced, well-maintained centrepin revolve to the speed of the river is a deep satisfaction in itself. A light, responsive rod is a joy to hold, to feel cut through the air or to bend into a lively fish.

The urge to fish has always been strong in man, and accordingly the history of fishing tackle stretches back thousands of years. Spears and arrows, nets and rocks: the earliest rods and lines have all led to the extraordinary creations of today. This is not the place to detail the history of fishing tackle over the centuries. Those of you who are interested should try to obtain a copy of *Fishing from the Earliest Times* by William Radcliffe. This amazingly scholarly work was published in 1921 and will give any details the historian might ask for. In a much more down-to-earth, modern book like this it is quite enough to remind you of the post-war tackle which many of us grew up with and to consider how far things have advanced in so short a time. Not that our early outfits were all that bad: the Industrial Revolution had provided

Old tackle is now very collectable.

many of the materials and much of the engineering knowledge to make tackle quite fine and precise. Victorian and Edwardian ingenuity had worked with these practicalities, and by the turn of this century some very efficient tackle was available.

Those of us fishing after 1950 were boosted by nylon lines, the pioneering design of Richard Walker and his circle, and the widening availability of fixed-spool reels. Soon there were to be glass rods as well as wooden and metal ones, and then even hollow glass to give exceptional power combined with lightness. Fishing was moving quickly towards the sophistication of today, though there were still advances to be made. Remember those reel-bail arms that thumped over like guillotines, the lines that broke at a fraction of their advertised strength, the hooks that blunted and bent and split shot that broke teeth like eggshells? Winter clothing tended to consist of a bri-nylon anorak and woollen gloves – if you were lucky.

Human beings are a strange bunch, and to some of them, fishing tackle has been more important than the fish it was designed to catch. Today we see the strange cult of the collector of vintage tackle – often characters who have never actually fished in their entire lives! See them at the important London auctions, where they handle tackle that was the pride and the joy of real anglers long gone.

Still, even these collectors reinforce the point that tackle can be very beautiful as well as coldly efficient. If you have any doubts, look at how the old creels mature into the colour of century oak or admire the pure artistry of a Victorian quill float. Ancient cane rods, too, acquire the lined, pitted character of a face out of a Hardy novel, and some old reels seem to revolve for ever, at least all day, with little more pressure than the brush of a butterfly wing.

Modern tackle has not the charisma of the hand-built pieces of yesterday. The craftsman has all but disappeared in a world of mass production and advanced machine tooling – though there are some notable exceptions whom we will meet in the course of this book. However, this does not inhibit the tackle mania of many: you can see them sitting like miniature mountains of electric blue, red or gold around the waterside with every possible accessory to hand. They sit on jumbo baskets with a battery of rods made up behind them and enough bait to feed the fish of the entire world. These men are like mobile human

tackle shops, and the possession of every latest piece of tackle is as important as the landing of the fish . . . or even more so. Just to have the tackle bright and new and gleaming satisfies their egos and their ambitions.

Conscious rebels exist: those who glory in the disarray of their gear and who delight in pulling the reel from the groundbait bucket and sticking the odd rodring back on with tape. Their floats look as though the cat has dragged them in, and it is not unusual to find a seriously repulsive deadbait long forgotten in their coat inside pocket . . . 'So that was the smell! I thought there was something worse than usual!' Such is the smelly rebel, but there is a more aristocratic one, who snootily describes the latest rod as good for growing beans upon and prefers to stick with his badly warped cane rod which probably came out of the Ark. A

A large show of antique tackle attracts an enthusiastic audience.

fixed-spool reel to this man is an abomination. Carbon is something you get from coal. You fish in a tie and tweeds rather than badges and polyester and if you must know the time, your watch really should be on a chain.

Of course, these groups are only on the fringe. Most of us are interested in tackle but not slaves to it. We see it as a very beautiful means to the all-important end of catching fish. If there are any golden rules, they are to choose tackle wisely, to prepare it and maintain it conscientiously and then forget it and think only of the fish, safe in the knowledge that your gear will do the job in both presentation and battle.

This is where the present book is planned to be of use. It is important to understand that the tackle industry today is worth millions of pounds. Many of the companies involved in it are international giants competing voraciously for markets that are bombarded with advertising material. The angler works hard for his money and his leisure time, and he cannot afford to buy unwisely – even though there are many temptations to do so. Capturing a certain fish or winning a prestigious match can, quite simply, make an angler's whole year. The wrong choice of tackle can, in a second, see all the possibilities disappear. If that hook should straighten, if that line should stretch, or if that rod has an ounce too little backbone then it is farewell to all the hopes and the dreams.

The problem in this vast, oversaturated market, is where to begin choosing the right tackle for the job. There is simply so much available, and all of it is made to sound so desirable, that mistakes are easy to make. In the following pages, experts in the world of tackle look at exactly what is needed for the thousand different jobs the angler will face over his career. At the end of several chapters, I do mention specific brand names and companies. When I do, the purpose is not to provide free advertising but to point the angler in the right direction in the tackle shop. Wherever possible I or the experts have tried to outline the type of things that you should look for in the tackle that you buy.

The book does not contain chapters on do-it-yourself or on tackle building. There are books available which study this in detail. I feel that this is an ever more specialized branch of the fishing world and its devotees are very few compared with years ago. You see, there is no longer the need that there used to be to design and to build special tackle. Such is the state of the industry today that whatever an angler needs is probably already commercially available. Also, the quality and finish is almost certain to be far higher than any amateur workman could possibly achieve. Make no mistake, there is superb tackle available today: what many anglers need is to understand it and to know what items to choose for their particular purposes.

1 Hooks

I make no apologies for beginning this book with the barbed subject of hooks! For as long as man has fished, the question of the hook has consumed him, and many patterns occurred, even to the minds of Bronze Age man; modern technology and ingenuity have taken this process a million miles further. The hook is vital to the catching of the fish – the hook, that is, and the type of line to which it is attached. A delicate rod and an efficient reel may be a tremendous bonus, but without the right combination of hook and line all will be lost.

The problem is compounded by the scores of different hook makes and patterns now on the market: make no mistake, hook manufacture in the 1990s is big business. If you think that there must be around a hundred million anglers throughout the world and then consider that each of those anglers probably buys on average 100 hooks a year, and you will end up with the sort of figure that is almost cosmic in its magnitude. The company that stakes a lion's share in that market is on the way to soaring profits. First, however, it has to get the product right and today there are many attempts at producing the perfect hook – most of which only serve to bewilder the poor buyer. For example, Saiko, Partridge, Drennan, Sunridge, Kamasan, Mustad, Nash, Gold Label, Owner, Marvic and Gardener, to name just a few, all make extensive ranges of hook! How do you choose? Then there are the colours . . . when do you want a red hook, a gold hook, a black or a bronze one? Do you need carbon wire, and if so, should it be fine, heavy or medium? Should your hooks be forged or made from steel? Should the shape be a round bend, a crystal bend or special bend? Should it have a wide or a narrow gape? Should it have a long shank, a short shank or a medium shank? Should it be a straight or a bent hook? Should the hook be eyed or spade end? And should the eye be out-turned?

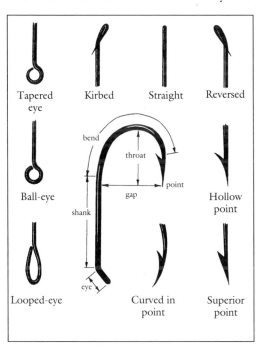

Tapered eye   Kirbed   Straight   Reversed

Ball-eye   bend   throat   point   gap   shank   Hollow point

Looped-eye   eye   Curved in point   Superior point

Hook terminology.

HOOKS

It is at times like this that a hook really has to measure up.

Should that hook be barbed, barbless, semi-barbed or a Starpoint? And how on earth should you attach the hook to the line? Should your knot be the blood-knot, the tucked blood-knot or the grinner knot? All this and we haven't really looked in any detail at carp hooks or the multitude of treble hooks on the market for pike or zander.

Indeed, the question of carp and pike hooks is so enormous that it is best to leave these to their respective chapters. The situation with general hooks is only a little easier. However, there are starters: recent research has shown that Drennan Hooks (along with its subsidiary, Kamasan) probably control around 80 per cent of the British hook market. This domination is probably based on several things: certainly Drennan's marketing is excellent, and even the glamorous hook boards seen in many tackle shops must attract

the buyer's attention. Furthermore, once an angler has settled on a particular make of hook, research tends to indicate that he sticks with it. He feels confident in the brand, and is understandably reluctant to change. Certainly it needs something dramatic to make him risk losing a fish for simple trial and error.

However, quite obviously, the hook has to be a good one in the first place. Drennan Hooks have certainly proved their worth time and time again over the last few years, and this is one occasion when I do not hesitate to use a brand name. In the big fish world, there is no doubt that the most popular hooks for many years have been the Drennan Super Specialist range in all their many sizes. Quite simply, these are some of the toughest, most rugged hooks that anglers have ever been able to buy, and it is very rare indeed to hear an angler blame his Super Specialist for letting him down. The design, the material and the attention to detail make this one of the great hook success stories of modern times. Times do not stand still, however, and Drennan have tried to improve on the Super Specialist. They now market the Starpoint range, which is even more technically advanced. The Starpoint name comes from the fact that this is a four-sided hook point. The four sides give the hook tremendous strength and the point now is almost impossible to blunt or to break under normal conditions. Also, it is claimed that penetration into the fish's mouth is greatly aided. The Starpoint hook also features the anti-eject bend shape. This is designed so that the point turns and pulls into the mouth of the fish if it tries to eject the hook. The sharp point lodges somewhere in the mouth almost immediately. Certainly, trials seem to suggest that there is a great deal of truth in the claim.

Drennan have also attempted to make one of the strongest hooks ever in this particular size range. The hooks are (for the technical) cryogenically tempered. This means that after the hooks have been made they are frozen to some incredibly low temperatures – certainly less than –100°C. This process rearranges the molecular structure of the metal and makes the hook as strong as possible.

The Starpoint and the Super Specialist hooks have been excellently designed, and it is no wonder that so many anglers use them; this does not mean, however, that other makes are inadequate or lacking. Both Partridge and Mustad to name just two, make excellent alternatives. Whichever brand of hook you decide upon, there are certain things to be borne in mind; for example the crystal-bend design tends to be stronger than the round-bend design. You can try this yourself with forceps: a hook with a crystal bend is stronger to gape – that is straighten out. However, round-bend hooks can be quite strong enough for many circumstances and

they allow a delicate bait to sit probably more happily on the hook. Casters, for example, are hooked very neatly on the round bend.

Length of shank is also important. A long-shanked hook is very useful if you are using delicate baits like bloodworm that can be threaded up the shank to some extent, and thus be given a little extra strength. You might also find a long-shanked hook useful for larger worms. A medium-shanked hook is more typically used for tougher baits like maggots or sweetcorn. I am rather suspicious of the long-shanked hook when it comes to fishing in very difficult situations. I suppose logically the strength of the hook should depend on the thickness and quality of the wire from which it is made. However, years of experience have tended to suggest that a long-shanked hook does gape more easily under pressure than a medium-shanked hook. My knowledge of physics is pretty elementary and I would not like to say why this happens in any technical detail . . . but it seems to do so at the waterside.

Most anglers are desperately aware of the importance of hook strength, and much of this is due to the thickness of the wire from which the hook is made. Also, the quality of that wire is important, and most of today's leading companies use the highest quality carbon steels in their manufacture. Penetration is of the utmost importance, and the Japanese have pioneered the process of chemical etching. This tends to make the points sharper than the more usual cut-etching system and the point is far less likely to be terminally damaged using this system. The technique is particularly useful for the small, fragile hooks that matchmen use.

There do not seem to be many areas left for hook development in the future. Even the colour of hooks has been well investigated. Drennan, again, was one of the leaders in this area when they brought out the gilt-coloured sweetcorn hook. The concept here was that the hook was close to the colour of the bait and would therefore be less visible. In the same way red hooks are now available, particularly in smaller sizes, for use with bloodworms or red maggots. Silver-coloured hooks are also available, and their flash gives them a fish-catching ability all of their own without any bait being needed at all. A silver hook, for example, jigged up and down in a shoal of small perch can often prove irresistible.

One factor of vital importance is the decision between spade-end hooks or eye hooks. Generally, spade-end hooks tend to be used by matchmen for their lightness and their forgiving way with small baits. A maggot on a small spade-end hook tends to fall through the water very easily indeed, whereas the same bait on an eyed hook of the same size can fall unnaturally enough to disturb the fish. This problem is not restricted to small fish in the match scene: on very clear waters I have seen large roach, for example, come very close to a hooked maggot or caster and examine it

minutely for five or six inches of its fall. They will reject it if there is anything suspicious about it. It is easy to forget that a big fish in clear water has excellent vision of what it is about to eat and the most minute thing that is wrong will alarm it. Of course, this is not nearly so critical in clouded water or at night but when conditions are on the fish's side, the hook choice has to be perfect. So, for most situations, I continue to use my eyed hooks, but there are occasions when a switch to a spade end is a wise move.

A frequent problem is that an angler needs the strongest hook that he can find but also the lightest, and the two properties rarely go together. The challenge set by tench, for example, in a shallow, clear, rich lake is a perfect example. You need a strong hook to hold these powerful fish away from weed and snags when they finally suck in the bait. But here is a snag: tench will often feed by drifting over the bed, sucking food from a distance of two or three inches into their mouths. Bait without the weight of the hook goes in naturally and easily, but bait tethered by the weight of the hook fails to rise in the same fashion. The tench is not really being selective and is not being alarmed: it is simply that the hook bait doesn't make it into its mouth. A lighter hook is obviously called for, but this is not easily found without forfeiting the strength required. The answer is either to make the bait itself more buoyant in some way (probably with a polystyrene insert) so that this neutralizes the weight of the hook, or to fit the hook itself with a piece of polystyrene (now commercially available in tiny segments) so that it is made much more weightless in the water.

Quite a while ago I used to teach, and one of the perks was to take the angling club out fly fishing as well as coarse fishing. What became apparent was that the boys who mastered everything began to catch fish, whereas those who made one or two mistakes

a) Make a loop and lay it against the hook shank leaving an end of about 2½in.

b) Wrap the free end around the loop about eight times and pass it through the loop. Moisten the knot.

c) Hold the free end and apply pressure to the hook-length so the knot slides tight.

Whipping knot for spade-end hooks.

Many fish will only take a hook that is balanced by the weight of the bait. Here the author inserts pieces of polystyrene into sweetcorn.

frequently caught nothing. Everything had to be 100 per cent correct: fly choice, fly presentation and fly movement had to be perfect or fish would simply not be caught. Now, in many coarse angling situations, you will find exactly the same thing. There are times when a river is in flood, for example, when hook choice is not that important, but there are many other times when the fish are in the swim and even feeding, and an angler has no indication of their interest. If everything is not absolutely correct, he will go home biteless and fishless, and not have a clue about what he was missing. That is why the hook is such an important consideration. Get the choice wrong and there are times when the day will be totally blank.

HOOKS TO LOOK OUT FOR

It is probably fair to say that Drennan hooks of one sort or another dominate the hook market at the moment. They are well marketed and attractively packaged, but above all they are strong and reliable and well priced. In the small sizes Kamasan (also marketed by Drennan) are proving very popular with match anglers. Partridge hooks are also very strong on the specialist scene, and some of the Mustad patterns are worth looking at. The carp world is very confusing but Drennan Star Point and Boilie hooks are worth a look. The various Owner rangers are attracting very wide attention and Kevin Nash makes some very strong Snag hooks.

2 Rods

By and large, the rods on the market today fall into three categories: float rods, feeder rods and specialist rods. Before we look at these in greater detail, let's just think of the basic standards which exist.

A float rod will be between 12 and 13ft long and weigh, if it is carbon, 6 to 8oz. If the rod is designed principally for stick-float fishing then a tip action will be the most popular, but if it is a waggler rod, then an all-through action is preferable. Remember, the tip action means that the bend or the play in the rod is restricted to the top section, whereas with an all-through action, there is movement from at least half-way down the rod. The handle will be of cork, cork looka-like or duplon. Most fishermen and rod builders prefer traditional cork. The rodrings may be lined, and if they are of the highest quality they will be made by Fuji or Seyo. Some rodrings do not have a lining and are made of a hard alloy. The lined rings, generally, protect lines that little bit more – a consideration that is very important when using very light breaking strains. Most float rods have a test curve of 8–16oz.

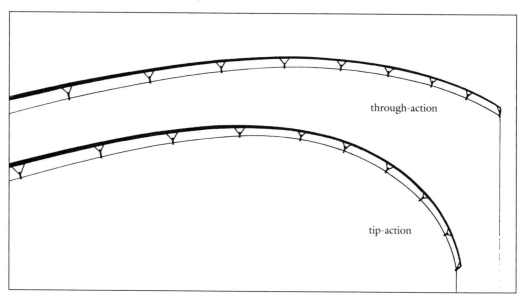

There are two basic rod actions.

A rod out over the Royalty fishery.

A feeder rod will typically be between 10½ and 12ft long. Its backbone will depend on the weight, the feeder and type of river it is expected to handle. So, for example, the Wye and Severn will probably demand a large feeder rod, whereas for on lakes or a river like the Wensum the lightest feeder rod will probably be quite adequate. A feeder rod should be able to take a variety of different tips, and certainly you should look for one which can handle a minimum of two with a capacity to take a whole line of them. This is important as conditions vary considerably. On average, a feeder rod will be expected to handle 3–4lb main line, but there are times when this will have to be stepped up to 6–8lb when barbel fishing, for example, on a heavy snaggy swim. It is important that the feeder rod has lined rings. The heavy terminal tackle puts a lot of pressure on the line and this will quickly cut grooves if the rings are not of the best quality. The good feeder rod will have the strength to cast the desired feeder the desired distance, but it will not lack a supple, precise action when playing the fish.

The specialist rods are either feeder or float rods upgraded for bigger fish and specialized roles. These are generally of a very high quality, but slightly stronger than the normal float rod would be. Lengths obviously vary depending on the style of fishing the rod is required to do, but most are between 11–13ft and probably the most common length for a carp rod is a 12ft rod in two pieces: two pieces rather than three tend to give a rod a better action. The length of a specialist rod is important, especially when it comes to distance fishing. If, for example, big fish are sought at distance on the feeder then a 13ft rod would probably be the desired weapon. Equally, if a long-distance carp rod is needed then its test curve will be at least 2½lb, it will have screw reel fittings and as few eyes as possible to cut down on line friction. However, remember with long-distance fishing that the diameter of line is very important. For example, 15lb line will only cast a limited distance because of the reduced speed through the rings, whilst 8lb line and a 3m shock leader will cast very much further with far greater effort.

RODS

It is a general rule that the more money you spend on a rod, the better the quality will be. Remember that carbon is an excellent material but it does come in different grades, and a poor carbon rod is not a very nice tool at all. When choosing a rod, always take the reels that you will be using along with you to the tackle dealer's. Fit them on to the proposed rod and see how they marry together. Choosing a rod is a very personal affair – do not be swayed by all the hype and advertising in the media today. Finally, let me explain that carp and pike rods are dealt with separately in their own chapters later in the book.

FLOAT RODS

One of the most important things about choosing a float rod is that it must be balanced. This concept is almost impossible to put into words, but basically the rod should not feel heavy in any way. If you pick the rod up from the floor it should rise cleanly without strain or pressure on your part. This sounds rather vague I know, but if you go to a tackle shop and try it on a whole range of rods, both cheap and expensive, you will begin to see what I mean. Also, and this is vital, never go to a tackle shop without taking your reel. The two should be firmly married together and be totally compatible. Obviously, lightness is a very important consideration because if the rod is heavy, you will tire or your float control will become less precise. Lightness today is not a real problem with the advent of carbon fibre but if the rod does not balance well with the reel then it will begin to feel heavy after a few hours. Lightness and slimness can be bracketed together and the slimmer the rod the better, for it will slice through the air more cleanly and will not present as much resistance when striking or when mending the line. Also it will not be nearly as affected by strong winds.

Unlike a leger rod, you are holding a float rod all the time and it should fit you like a glove. The handle, therefore, is very important. It should be slim and almost certainly made of cork: in my eyes there is no better material. This handle should be around 22–23in long for most adults. Anything much longer or shorter should probably be rejected.

The rings on a float rod are very important as they do take a tremendous amount of line travel over the years. The market leaders are probably Fuji, whose products are light and hard wearing and allow very easy line passage. If a rod has cheap rings they will probably be heavier and spoil the precise action of the rod. They will become grooved easily and will have to be replaced more often. Even worse, a groove on the line can fray it and lose a potentially invaluable fish. Rings made of titanium are now appearing more and more regularly, and this will probably be the only material used in the near future.

The next thing to consider is the length of the rod, and often you see anglers struggling to control a float with a rod that is less than 10ft long – a hopeless task. Most float rods now are built between 12–13ft long and if you choose one shorter than this, control is almost certain to suffer. There are longer rods now available as carbon fibre is so light, and a 15ft rod, for instance, will give you extra control over the float. Also, that extra foot or two will mean an amazingly increased amount of line pick-up on the strike. However, long rods are very expensive and as usual you have to strike the balance between cost and efficiency.

There are basically two float rod actions. The first type, which is marginally more common, is a forward action or a tip action. Such a rod bends at the tip as you would expect, whilst the middle and butt sections remain comparatively rigid. This type of action allows a rapid strike and is perfect for close-in control and fishing the stick float. It also plays a

A slim tench float rod has done the business.

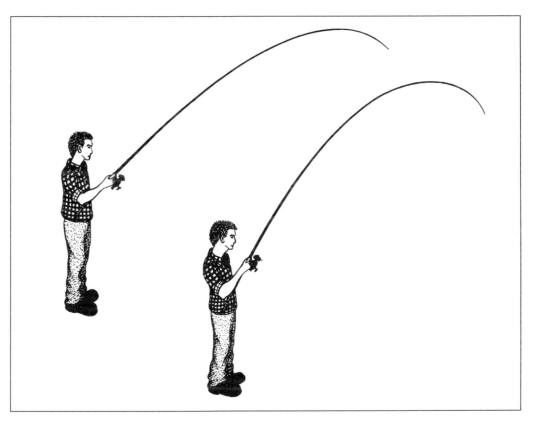

Two stages of rod action.

fish very firmly and directly and is ideal for keeping a big fish from a snag. The second type of action is a more all-through or softer action. The middle section tends to bend along with the top section, and the rod probably feels a little floppy by comparison. Certainly it is not the precision tool of the tip-action rod alone. These rods are perfect for use with a waggler when you have to cast a distance and move a lot more line through the water when you strike. This rod, being softer, means that you do not bump nearly so many fish off the hook when you strike.

Most top-ranking float anglers possess the two actions which should deal with virtually every float-fishing situation that you are likely to meet. Two rods, however, are obviously expensive and it is probably best to start with the tip-action rod if finances are in any way tight – as they are almost certainly bound to be. As usual, aim for the most expensive rod you think you can afford: the money is virtually always well spent although there are some excellent budget rods on the market.

Float Rods to Look Out For

At the top of the range, Drennan, Tri-Cast, Browning, Normark and Jan Porter all make some wonderful rods. Cheaper rods can be purchased from Shakespeare, Silstar, Dam, Sunridge and Daiwa. You do get what you pay for to a certain extent, but many of the lower-priced rods are well balanced, delicate and very light. The Shakespeare Equalizer is one that has been particularly well reviewed.

QUIVER-TIP RODS

I remember well talking to John Wilson in 1975 about the concept of quiver-tip rods. At that time, believe it or not, it was impossible to buy one ready made-up, and he suggested that I purchase a glass-walled Avon rod and insert a solid, fine glass tip into the top section. The idea was that it would be perfect for those large, shy-feeding Wensum roach. Well, the project went ahead, the rod was built and it was an absolute, utter failure. It certainly registered bites, but hitting them was an entirely different matter. I should think, on average, that I connected with 10 per cent of bites that I saw and on a river like the Wensum, the rod was a recipe for suicide. Never has the importance of rod design been more strongly underlined for me personally. If a quiver-tip is not designed properly, it is absolutely useless. What was wrong with that early Avon prototype? For a start, the tip was too stiff and the roach tended to feel it and let go of the bait too quickly to make a successful strike. Probably just as disastrous was the fact that the quiver-tip insert and the rod were

Tippexing a quiver-tip white helps with visibility at dawn and dusk.

Deceptively casual, Roger Miller waits for the tip to quiver!

totally out of balance with each other. There was no real harmony between the two: the rod was a hybrid and it reacted in a disjointed fashion. If a fish were hooked the quiver-tip bent round at a crazy angle and the main rod itself hardly moved at all.

I mention this early attempt to highlight the fact that quiver-tip design has moved ahead in leaps and bounds over twenty years. The main impetus for this has been the swim-feeder: now most legering is done with a swimfeeder, probably, and the quiver-tip rod is the perennial partner. With the help of computers and modern, high-tech materials it is now possible to buy carbon quiver-tip rods that weigh less than 6oz and still have tremendous power and backbone. A major advance has been the development of selections of push-in tips that give great flexibility to any

quiver-tip made today. All these tips can now be matched to the parent rod and are engineered to a predetermined test curve. These are incredibly delicate, precise tools correct to a fraction of a thousandth of an inch.

Virtually every major rod-making company constructs a range of quiver-tips and the problem lies in choosing the correct one. All of them will do the job and once again the question tends to centre upon money. Obviously, to some degree, the more money you spend the better the quality of the rod. Remember that if the rod is to be used for fishing a swim-feeder, it will need to be robust. Swim-feeder fishing really takes it out of tackle more than any other method. Check particularly the standard of the rodrings. The best rods will probably be equipped with Seymo or Fuji or something similar: space-age materials that resist line abrasion for years. Buy poor rodrings and you will find they are grooved within a couple of sessions and line wear is terrific. Rod diameter is also very important: the thinner the rod, the lighter it is likely to be, the more easily it will cut through the air on the strike and the cast, and the less likely it is to be affected by the wind.

A rod which can take a wide variety of quiver-tips is also to be recommended. Quiver-tips of around 1–2oz test curve are pretty standard but it is possible to find them lighter or quite a lot heavier. The standard colour of most quiver-tips is either neon orange or red. I have been told by one major manufacturer that the public do not like white. I fail to understand why this is the case because white shows up so much better under most conditions and is of course, much easier to see as darkness approaches.

If you are to take quiver-tipping or feeder fishing seriously, one medium-actioned rod and one heavy feeder rod will probably see you through most situations. The heaviest of feeder rods will cast a 4oz loaded feeder way over 60 or 70 yards. The butt section will be powerfully built and it will probably have a faster than usual taper with plenty of power around the middle. The rod will be at least 12ft long so it can be held high in the air and keep as much line as possible off the water – an important consideration when fishing at great distances in heavy flows. Such a rod is perfect for the type of water for which it is designed, but is not particularly adaptable. You will find a light to medium feeder rod much more suited to most fishing situations.

Very recently, a new type of rod, for me at least, was put into my hands: a Drennan Light

A torch beneath the rod highlights the quiver-tip and shows up the slightest movement.

Bomb rod. In some ways this was like a quiver-tip rod but the slim, sensitive tip was actually built into the rod and not pushed in. When I first held it, I immediately realized that this gave the rod an extreme sensitivity. I took the rod away and within two days was using it for some very shy-biting roach. The results were absolutely amazing: a bite would simply go on for ever and it seemed as though normally shy fish would never let go, even if I did not bother to strike! I then took the rod up to Scotland to fish for grayling. Again, the results were astounding: the grayling bites were magnified to a huge extent and became virtually unmissable. The rod, despite being very light and delicate, coped extremely well with fish up to 2½lb in ranging water. Certainly, for most of my delicate quiver-tip fishing in the future, especially when a feeder is not required, the Light Bomb rod will be my choice of weapon. This is one of those situations when I feel a brand name should be mentioned, and I have no hesitation in doing so. Obviously, the Light Bomb rod will also cope with a small feeder or feeder link for shy-biting fish in cold conditions. All in all, it is a most versatile and willing tool.

The Swing-Tip Option

It is a fact that the quiver-tip is more flexible and has a greater variety of uses than the swing-tip, but that does not mean that swing-tipping should be ignored. The swing-tip can detect bites on the rod more obviously and shows up a developing bite more clearly. It is important to realize that the tension on the line does not increase as the bite builds up, and therefore the fish is less likely to drop a bait on the swing-tip than it is on the quiver. Also, a swing-tip is more easily seen as the light begins to fade or in poor light conditions. However, the swing-tip is more affected by wind, is more prone to tangling on the cast and is difficult to fish in fast-running water. Also, really tentative bites do not show up quite as well.

There are several different types of swing-tip and most have screw-in attachments that can be fixed to a rod with a compatible end rig. The traditional swing-tip is simply made from one length of very stiff nylon, but now there are different varieties made for different conditions. For example, there is a heavy metal swing-tip for strong winds or running water and another one with a very stiff link that makes the swing-tip stable in high winds. Obviously, the softer the link to the rod, the more sensitive the swing-tip is likely to be. Most general legering rods of 10–12ft prove perfect for marriage with a swing-tip, and the bomb or feeder should be cast out with a very gentle pendulum-type action or tangles can result. It pays to have the spool absolutely topped up with line so that friction is kept to a minimum.

Quiver-Tip Rods to Look Out For

Most major companies build quiver-tip rods, and the Daiwa range has won great acclaim. For my money, however, and for that of many specialist anglers, there is little to beat the Drennan range of light, medium and heavy feeder rods. These seem exquisitely made and perfectly balanced for the bigger fish angler.

RODS FOR TOUCH LEGERING

There are times when it is possible to become blinkered and try to use a quiver-tip rod in all situations. I am thinking particularly of river fishing at night for barbel and chub. Very often, under these conditions, it is better to touch leger than to rely on a visual indication. I would like to quote from that classic book of the 1970s, *The Big Fish Scene,* edited by

Frank Guttfield. In his chapter on barbel, John Everard wrote:

'When fishing in the dark I invariably hold the rod. Barbel bites can vary considerably from a strong wrenching pull to a small positive pull of half an inch on the rod tip. At other times you can feel a sawing sensation on the rod tip. Generally, though, bites are positive and quite easily hooked. I never strike hard unless fishing at a great distance. A strong steady pull is all that is required to set the hook. A wild strike will only result in line breaking. It is noticeable that day time bites are more violent and usually consist of a strong pull. It would appear that the barbel can see the bait and will grab it as if in competition with other fish. Night time

A perfect swim to touch leger. Notice how the rod is pointed at the bait.

bites too are very positive but more often consist of smaller pulls that are sometimes only just noticeable. The "sawing" type bites I mention can sometimes be felt at night too. I think that the feeding barbel will descend on the bait, swallowing it on the spot.'

So, for extra sensitivity and to avoid disturbing the swim, especially during clear water conditions, it is probably better to touch leger when possible. You can, of course, touch leger with the quiver-tip rod you have been using through the daylight hours, but this is not the perfect tool. The problem is that a good quiver-tip rod will be festooned with eyes and each one of these will reduce the 'feel' that is so vital to this particular method. What you really need for a touch legering rod is not too many eyes at all and for those that do exist to be large, not worn in any way and even, perhaps, slightly greased. That way friction is cut down and you will feel most of what is happening at the hook end of the gear.

The style of rod rather depends on the river you are fishing, the swim and the strength of the fish, but generally the old Avon-type affair is the one to aim for. Probably the rod will have a test curve of around 1½lb – give or take a few ounces – and possibly be somewhere in the region of 11ft long. Lightness is essential, for you will be holding the rod for many hours and you do not want weariness to creep in or you will lose concentration and the efficiency of the method will be reduced. For this reason, the most modern rods often make the best touch-legering tools. They also have great precision and the kind of sensitivity that can only help this very precise method. A reasonably short handle is also a bonus as you can tuck it neatly under your arm without it protruding and becoming a nuisance in the darkness.

The art of touch legering is more than half-forgotten today, probably because of the near

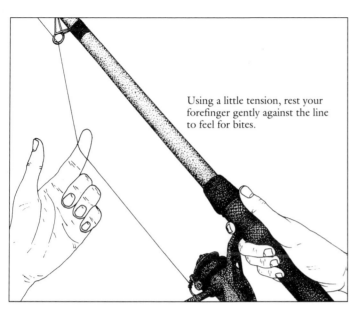

Touch-legering.

Using a little tension, rest your forefinger gently against the line to feel for bites.

perfection of quiver-tip rods. Indeed, it is very rare to see anglers touch leger even after dark, and a brief word on the method could be of use. As far as I am concerned the important thing is to have the line resting over either the index or middle finger so that any pressure on it can be felt at once. Obviously, it pays to point the rod as directly towards the bait as you possibly can so there is a direct pull to that all-feeling finger! Some of the bites will almost pull your hand up to the rodring and there is no mistaking these, but not all taking barbel and chub are quite as positive. Very often you will feel a type of tingling or a series of sharp pulls that could almost be mistaken for wind on the line. For this reason alone, touch legering demands a great deal of concentration and I find it preferable to fish alone as even quiet conversation tends to distract me and a bite can be missed.

John Everard made the point about a gentle strike, and this is very pertinent. A lot of touch legering is done close in under your own bank and a wild strike at a big fish under the rod tip will result in disaster. For this

reason, I rarely choose the Double Strength type line for this work and prefer something with a bit more give and resilience. For the same reason a rod with a certain amount of forgiveness is also a good idea. As always, choose the strongest hook that you can find and are happy with.

LURE RODS

Lure expert Charlie Bettell has his say:

'An ultra lightweight through-action lure rod can make the smallest of fish a pleasure to catch. When lure fishing solely for small fish (perch, chub, small pike and the like), it pays to own such a rod. For lightweight lure work (lures of ⅜oz or less) I use my 8ft and 8ft 6in American Lami Glass rods. For casting small lures and catching small fish, a Lami Glass rod is in a class of its own. When lure fishing for big fish though, I use a heavier type of rod. For the last seven years of lure fishing, I have also been using a 9ft 6in leger rod. I use the

Barry Rickards (on the left here) has done more than anybody else to pioneer lure fishing.

rod for my general lure fishing, casting small and large lures with it. The rod is capable of handling any size fish, but it does struggle to cast big lures. The action of my leger lure rod is top action when playing a small fish, and through action when playing fish of about 5lb-plus, the main point being that it bends when playing any size of fish. I have never found another blank like it for lure fishing. The blank is very thin walled (an early carbon type) and the rod weighs virtually nothing. A long day's lure fishing using the rod and my Abu Cardinal 4 reel (290g/10.2oz) has no effect on my arm in the slightest. The rod and reel are, in fact, in perfect balance.

What is the perfect rod/reel balance? I consider the perfect balance (weightwise) to be when you can balance the rod and reel on one finger just in front of the reel foot or very close to it. Most of the thicker-walled (stronger) rods of today tend to be a bit too front heavy. Front heavy unbalanced rods are no good for casting small lightweight lures about all day.

It was Pete Rogers, seen here holding a lovely ferox trout, who taught me the importance of having a sensitive lure rod when trolling.

Steve Burke of the Perch Fishers uses a quiver-tip lure rod (for perch and pike) just like the French do when lure fishing for zander. A quiver-tip rod is very sensitive to the lightest of knocks. With some types of lure rods you are left scratching your head after a pull on the rod! Was that a knock? Perhaps it was just weed! Yes, it must have been weed! Or was it? When using a quiver-tip rod you don't have those niggly little thoughts; you know whether or not it was a fish bite or a weed bite. The French use a quiver-tip rod, as I said, when lure fishing for zander, which is far more sensitive for spotting the zander's very light tugs at their lure! They even go a stage further than their rod for bite detection. They found that zander wouldn't generally dive downwards (creating rod pull) on hitting their lure, so they came up with the idea of using glowing line to spot the bite. On retrieve, they watch the line where it enters the water and as soon as the line moves north, south, east or west (or any other compass degree), they strike. They have great success using the method, so I've been told.'

SPLIT CANE RODS

There is no doubt that split cane rods are undergoing some sort of renaissance at present. Indeed, these excellent weapons seem to appear on rather a cyclical basis. For example, in the late 1960s when we were all getting a bit fed up with hollow glass rods, split cane made a strong reappearance. In the same way now, as we move into the late 1990s and are getting quite used to the properties of carbon, split cane offers something new and rather more characterful. Of course, it is more difficult to justify split cane against carbon than it ever was in the glass fibre days. Glass rods by and large were a pretty drab lot; most were hopeless and nearly all were nasty. Picking up

a glass rod was frequently like trying to wield a huge sponge – and the same certainly cannot be said of the carbon rods of today, which are light, precise and a joy to behold. Still, there are those that prefer split cane . . .

Split cane rods have been with us for around one hundred and fifty years and certainly up until World War Two they were considered *the* rods to own. Thousands upon thousands were made, including such classics as the Kennet Perfection, the Wallis Wizard and the B. James Avons and Mark IVs. Some of these rods are even seen on the bank today and are quite capable of doing sterling service despite being several decades old.

Edward Barder lives and works in Wiltshire, and is one of today's young craftsmen still working in split cane. For a while he worked at Hardy's, constructing both cane and carbon rods but when he decided to go out on his own, he chose to specialize in the former. Long conversations with him have painted some important pictures of what to look for in the world of split cane rods. An immediate point he makes is that we should not assume that any cane rod of age today is worth a fortune. We must remember that thousands were made and from the 1930s in particular, they were constructed on a mass basis. The problem is that it is many years since the tackle shops stocked cane rods, and now customers do not know what to look for: the obvious tendency is to think that every old cane rod is worth a lot of money when it is not. Everything hexagonal is not marvellous. There is a lot of rubbish sold through the press advertisement pages, at auctions, in antique shops and at car boot sales. Just as there is much second-rate carbon today, so there is a lot of poor split cane available now to the angler who does not know what to look for.

One of the big questions that faces Edward in his trade is explaining to people that cane still has it place, that it is not a living relic and

Chris Yates, an angler of many parts, still uses his old split cane rods.

that it is practical. The simple fact is that split cane rods are different from carbon – not necessarily worse or better, simply different. Like anything in the fishing world, split cane has its own advantages and disadvantages – although Edward adds that he has never met anyone who does not like using split cane rods under the right conditions.

Whilst it is possible to make a cane rod do anything from beach casting to big-game fishing to a long-trotting rod or a long-distance carp rod, there are jobs that carbon does much better. Edward considers that cane is a tremendous material when weight is not that important: so, for example, if you are looking for a long float rod that you will need to hold all day, it is better to choose carbon than cane (though obviously you will get used to the

weight in time – our grandfathers did, after all). But, generally, cane comes into its own when you want it to do something a little more precise or when you do not have to hold it for a long time. In the fly-fishing world cane is often considered to be a better material for rods up to 9ft in length. Cane can present a nymph or a dry fly at close quarters in a beautiful way. Because the cane loads under its own inertia the caster does not have to put too much energy into the motion: as a result he puts his line down more delicately and at a slower speed.

In the same way, split cane can be used in specialized areas of coarse fishing with great effect. Remember, cane is a softer material which provides a cushioning effect for any hooked fish, so often it is possible to get away with lighter tackle than carbon permits. Therefore, when choosing split cane for coarse fishing, think of those times when you will only need a rod of up to around 11ft so that weight does not become a problem. Equally, cane is best when you do not have to hold the rod all the time, so it makes a perfect legering rod for barbel or for chub in rivers or for carp and tench at short to medium range.

There are two real reasons why you should consider using cane. Firstly, there is little doubt that cane is more responsive than carbon when a fish is hooked. Most people agree about this: there is a lot more life in a split cane rod when you are playing a fish than there is in a carbon rod. Carbon is very, very efficient but it does not give out the excitement that there is in cane. Of course, this cannot be proved and you have to take the word of many hundreds of people for it. Why can this happen? Well, Edward says, part of the answer lies in the material and part of it in the shape. And, remember too, that split cane is solid and somehow the vibrations travel through a solid rod more consistently. One thing to realize is that in a cane rod, all the fibres run longitudinally along the rod right to the hand itself. This means that all the stresses of a plunging fish are transmitted to you. The vibrations can be lost if they are travelling down an inert, hollow tube. Remember, we are not fishing for a living but for enjoyment and anything that increases this enjoyment should be considered.

The second reason for choosing cane is all about enjoyment. Carbon rods are big business these days, and are mass produced in huge factories, often in the East. Even the individual rod makers still order their blanks from huge corporations and make their own individual modifications. Split cane, on the other hand, is a much more personal material. Wander into the workshop of a split cane rod maker and you realize that you are not looking at any

bland, black tubing. You can see a great deal has been done to the raw cane – even if you don't understand what. A man like Edward Barder gains a great deal of satisfaction from his rod making and this in some way seeps out to the customers that enjoy his work. Edward began by repairing one of his father's old rods when he was 16 years old. From that first step, he took to reading old books and talking to ancient, retired tacklemakers in the south. Bit by bit he picked up their knowledge and soon his business developed. His customers realize that this knowledge is deep and inherited and the aesthetic appeal is enormous. Indeed, the look of a split cane rod has always been important: B. James realized this very important fact when the company decorated their rods with a host of intermediate whippings. These

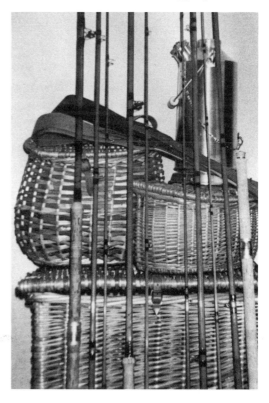

Split cane and creels – a lovely combination.

whippings offer nothing in terms of strength and simply add weight and prevent good casting in wet weather. They were simply added for their appearance, to appeal to the customer's eye and to make them feel that the rod was in some way superior.

The feel of the split cane rod is, to me, its most important benefit, but I can appreciate the aesthetics as well. After all, there are long hours of inactivity in any angler's life, and it is rather pleasant to while away the time looking at a beautiful rod rather than a drab one. Also, in life there are such considerations as quality and the personal touch. Inspector Morse with his Jaguar is one popular example of this, and the split cane rod certainly possesses quality and character.

The modern-day split cane user has two choices: he can either go to a man like Edward and order a new split cane rod to his exact specification or he can look around the sales and try to find a good antique rod. If the latter course is chosen, Edward offers some essential pointers so that money is not wasted on eleven feet of old and rotting rubbish. Firstly, examine the corners of each section – the sharp bits! If there are corners with gaps, chips or black lines, avoid the rod. These will mean either that the rod was not well planned in the first place so that the stripes did not fit together well, or that the glue has failed. The old rods were built with animal glue which can disintegrate if damp creeps in. In rare cases, damage to the corners of the rod can mean that the rod has been subjected to excessive stress and has begun to delaminate. This is rare, but any rod showing these imperfections should be avoided.

The straightness of the rod is of some importance. Most split cane rods when used to any degree will sag. They all do even under their own weight and that of the rings. Turn the rod over on its side either to the left or the right and if the sag is not drastic, do not worry

too much. Providing the rod is fairly straight, says Edward, then you are reasonably safe to go ahead with the purchase. Avoid rods with 'S' bends, dog legs, kinks or obvious cracks. Another thing to look for is dark blotches on the cane. These can mean that the varnish has chipped and the cane has been exposed to moisture. The blotches can sometimes be in the cane but if they look blurred, like a water mark, damp has got into the bamboo and probably upset the natural resins that hold the fibres together. The main resin is a form of starch called lignin, and if this is reduced or harmed the cane can be brittle and will suddenly snap under pressure.

Ferrules, according to Edward, are crucial. They are often worn with a lot of play in them that produces a knocking noise when the rod is waggled. The ferrules can be replated, but this is expensive and generally new ferrules are needed. This is not a difficult job for anything like an experienced rod builder. However, if the ferrule has started to separate from the cane this is a different matter altogether: it will probably mean that moisture has crept in and if pressure is put on a specific point, the rod will not be up to bearing the stress. There is also the worry that the split cane has been used to fit a ferrule. B. James actually committed this sort of malpractice towards the end of their great run. It seemed that they had a lot of ferrules to use up and the hexagonal point of the rod was turned into a circle to fit the ferrule. The outer fibres were removed and this is where the strength lies – not in the inner pinch. Therefore, always check the ferrules as carefully as you possibly can.

Varnish is also very important. A lot of rods can look structurally sound, but if the varnish is gone, there can be problems. If the rod appears to have been without varnish for a long time, there can be big trouble as moisture will probably have seeped in. If you know the owner and the background of the rod and it appears that the rod has only been taken out in warm weather, for example, and kept in a warm, dry attic, this might not be a problem. But, unless you know its background, avoid a de-varnished rod.

Up to the 1970s all rodrings were made of plain, mild steel, sometimes painted with chrome. This bright chrome was porous and allowed atmospheric moisture to get through and to rust the metal (you only have to think of old car-bumpers). The rings were also soft as well as prone to rust. Therefore, any rod built before the 1970s will almost certainly need re-ringing.

Many earlier rod makers suffered from a particular mania: attempting to preserve the colour of silk whippings with various different types of material. PVA wood glue and cellulose dope, known as banana oil, were often used. These flattened the fibres and sealed the whipping to some extent, and probably helped to preserve the colour. The problem was that they did in time go yellow and were not flexible. Also – and this is vital – they broke up and lifted away the varnish from the area. This process, of course, allowed the moisture to penetrate and proved the demise of many rods. So, if the varnish around the rings is yellow, cracking and lifting then beware of the rod as there could be trouble deep within it.

Finally, it is tempting to go only for the well-known makers of old rods – for example, Hardy's or Alcocks or James. It is important to remember that all split cane rod makers created very good rods, but the biggest makers did tend to produce more duds. It was inevitable – a simple law of statistics. The smaller makers could be more careful and fewer rods crept out that were below standard. The maker, therefore, is not really very significant and much more important is the condition of the old rod. For example, Edward says, some Wallis Wizards are brilliant and yet some are absolute horrors.

Considering all this, perhaps it is wise to go to one of the modern makers. Many people do, and that is why Edward has at least six or eight months' work lying ahead of him at any one time. Talking to him is a most enjoyable experience, for here is a man who really gets a thrill out of creation. Perhaps this excitement is transmitted into both the design and the product, and is picked up by the angler. Certainly all his customers speak of getting a thrill from the rods that they order and, of course, the rods do not fail; Barder rods have a list of whoppers to their credit, and have never once been known to let the angler down when it mattered. Making cane rods is hard work. The bamboo that grows on the Chinese hillsides can be 60ft tall and 6in in diameter. It is a hard, resilient material and reducing it to a precise instrument is a tough job. Indeed, at the end of the day, Edward can be quite exhausted. Fortunately, building split cane rods today brings plenty of interesting projects his way. He is constantly learning of better ways to make the rods, and meeting new people with new ideas. Also, one rod is never the same as the one before it (unless he is making a matching pair), so that everything has that sense of individuality. Split cane rod building is an art: in the old days an apprentice would have to study for ten years before being allowed to make a piece of cane fit for a customer. It is that type of learning and care that goes into split cane rods and Edward himself loves the end product. This love is appreciated by many – a growing number who search for something a little different in these days of mass-produced, mass-marketed equipment.

POLES

Everyone knows that for the match angler a pole is an extremely important piece of equipment. The rod and running line offer no-where near as much in terms of speed or delicacy of bait presentation, and many of our matches today are won without a normal rod even being assembled. Despite all this, I still do not know a specialist angler who owns one. No, that's wrong . . . I do! It was way back in the mid 1970s that a particular swim on the Wensum seemed almost impossible to fish. A combination of bankside cover and currents made a tiny area of the most juicy swims virtually impregnable. I mentioned the problem to John Wilson and in his inimitable way, he managed to sell me a pole to tackle the job. I went down to the river fired with excitement. I knew there were roach in the area, for I had seen them topping, and now all I needed to do was get the bait into their pre-cise bastion. Of course, I had never wielded a pole before and it was obviously a mistake to set out to catch big fish in a difficult area with-out any practice or experience behind me. Things, I can see now, just *had* to go wrong. And so they did.

Despite a fairly brisk wind, I was able to flick the float out over reeds under the alder bush-es into the exact piece of crease that I so far been unable to reach. The float dallied there for a minute and then wanted to drift away down with the current but with the 20ft pole,

Pole-fishing accessories are big business today.

I was able to hold it back and keep it exactly where I wanted it. Two minutes later, it had gone! The roach was definitely a good one and plugged away all over the river without me having much idea how to play it. It got off. So did the next four. The last fish I got almost to the bank, where it rolled – 2lb 12oz at least, and then it waved farewell with its dorsal! The pole that day had hooked me five fish and lost me five fish, and I was in despair. That hap-pened almost twenty years ago, and I have not taken the pole out since – except to clear the odd blocked drain!

You can see, therefore, that I am hardly qual-ified to talk about the choice of poles. Frank Russell of Wotsits Tackle Centre in Notting-ham definitely is. Frank probably helps more people to choose their pole than any other per-son in the course of a year. The range of Wot-sits' tackle is absolutely enormous and if anybody should know about poles, it is Frank. Here is what he has to say.

'A pole is probably the most expensive item any angler will buy, so you want to make sure that you buy the right one. Before you buy, decide exactly what you want the pole to do. Do you want a light pole that you can fish at 12½m on the canal, or do you only need a strong 9m pole for big chub on a small river? Have a look around on the bank and see if you can spot another angler using something that looks to be just what you need. If so, talk to him, ask if he has had any problems and what he thinks of the product. Has he had any experience of the availability of spares and back up from the man-ufacturer? You must also decide how much you want to spend and whether you are going to buy new or second-hand. However, for the purpose of this piece I will assume you are buy-ing new. (There do seem to be some good sec-ond-hand offers around, but make sure you do not buy someone else's problems as spare sec-tions can be expensive.)

The main thing to remember when buying a pole is that generally you get what you pay for, and competition between manufacturers and dealers at the moment is making pole prices better value than any other item of tackle. Buy the best that you can afford now and you should get a really good quality pole that you won't need to update in six months' time. Some manufacturers update models almost every year, so some good bargains can be obtained by buying a discounted model. Just because it does not feature in the current catalogue does not mean that it is no longer any good. Some of these are less than half price and spares are usually available for several years – but do check on this.

Think carefully about the maximum length of pole that you will need. Ask other anglers on the bank what length of pole they are using and whether it is long enough for their purposes. There is no point in buying a 14m pole if you will never use a pole longer than 11m as you will be paying for the extra section when you could be paying the extra for a lighter and stiffer pole. If you cannot be certain about the longer lengths it may be worth considering a pole that you can extend at a later date because as materials have improved, manufacturers have started to design poles at the longer lengths of say 14m and sell them from 11m.

The weight of a pole and how it feels in the hand is important. All manufacturers list the weight of their pole, but this is only a rough guide to quality. The balance of that weight is much more important than the weight itself, and the only way to check that is to handle the pole at full length and compare it with other poles in the same price, length and weight bracket that you have set yourself. Do not forget also that although a lighter pole will feel much nicer, it may not handle so well in the wind or with a fish attached as a slightly heavier, more robust pole does. Some ultra-light poles are absolutely unfishable on all but windless days. You won't find that out when you handle a pole in a showroom so ask advice.

You have to consider next the question of joints. There are two types of joints on poles: these are either put-in or put-over joints, and people are confused about which is which. Put over is when you are putting sections nearest the tip over or on to sections nearest the butt; in other words, putting thin sections on to thicker sections. Put in is, therefore, when you are putting sections nearest the tip into sections nearest the butt. It does not really matter which way they are as both designs have some advantages to offer. Put-over joints tend to be easier to use as you can see what you are doing better when putting the joint together. Also, these joints just go further as the joints wear, but put-in joints can, after considerable use, actually push inside the next section. (Looking after your pole and protecting the joints can avoid this.) Put-in poles usually have slimmer sections and are quite stiff, well-balanced poles. Whichever the type of joint you choose will not make that much difference once you get used to it and if you like the pole, don't let the joints put you off.

The action of the pole or how it works on the bank has also got to be considered. A lot of rubbish is talked about the action of poles and you should think about the action that would suit you. We see that different areas tend to prefer different actions but that may be because the locals are all using a certain action or even model and winning with it, so everyone else copies them. Some poles are ultra stiff and rely entirely on the elastic to play the fish, whereas others have after-tip sections that give a cushion as well as the elastic. Be careful that you do not confuse the soft tip action with sloppiness, which is what you do not want. Good-quality poles should strike and recover quickly, even if the pole has a softer action. If you do make a mistake and buy too stiff a pole, you may find that you "bump" off a few fish on the strike (or perhaps the pole is a bit too quick for the way you fish). A softer tip might fit and cure the problem. Or, vice versa, you may have bought soft action and find that you need something a little quicker or beefier.

Having decided what you want the pole to do, and armed yourself with any information you have managed to amass, visit a reputable dealer who stocks a good range of poles. Explain what you want, how much you want to spend and ask to compare any poles from the same range side by side and – this is most important – at full length. What you are looking for is to determine the action. It is stiff or sloppy; are the joints the type you prefer? (Remember, put-over joints are usually more popular, but put-in joints tend to make a slimmer, stiffer pole.) Is the pole the proper length that you need? Is it light enough for you to handle but strong enough to do the job? Do you get a spare top set? Can it be extended if you want it to be? Are spares available easily and does it feel comfortable to you? Remember you are the one who has got to use it, and if it does not feel right after ten minutes at a tackle dealer's, it is going to feel awful after a couple of hours on the bank. If you find a pole that fits all these criteria and does not mean taking out a second mortgage, you will have done very well because most people have to compromise to a certain extent. You cannot expect to get a 14m pole that is as stiff as a poker, as light as a feather, comes with two top kits and an extension to 16½m for a song. They do not exist. I remember a top angler saying several years ago that a top-class fishing rod would cost five weeks'

wages. Today, the rods and poles are much better quality, and a top-class rod is only one week's wages, while a top-class pole is only four weeks' wages. Tackle today is good value.

Finally, do not forget to insure your tackle. Tackle theft is a growth area at the moment and you will be surprised how the value adds up. Many firms sell tackle insurances, surely a wise investment when you are considering buying a pole with such enormous value.'

What Frank says about insurance is well worth bearing in mind: fishing tackle is expensive, and is an obvious magnet for thieves. Everything suggests theft of tackle is becoming more and more common; from cars, from sheds and even on the river bank itself. To lose a whole set of tackle is mentally and economically disastrous but adequate insurance does at least help to soften the blow. Sadly, because of the number and size of claims, many insurance companies are scrapping simple tackle policies. Now, the only certain way of getting cover is by extending your house contents insurance policies. All household insurance policies carry an all-risks section that provides cover away from home – so make sure your tackle is insured in this category. Rates obviously vary. Anglers should talk to the company who insures their home contents first as they are likely to get a better deal by adding on fishing tackle to their other possessions. Another advantage of keeping all your cover with one company is that you also get liability cover. If, for example, you caught someone's eye with your hook, caused damage and were sued, you would automatically be covered for personal liability of at least £500,000.

3 Reels

It is quite possible to catch good fish, even big ones, without a reel at all – ask any pole angler. However, for longer casting, something on which to store line is essential. The storage drum, for after all, that is all a reel is, need not even be on the rod. Many Third World fishermen simply wind something like twine

Part of the range of reels available today.

around a thick stake or rock and pull it off as they need it. In the hands of an expert fisherman, this primitive type of reel can be surprisingly effective.

Very efficient centrepins and multipliers were built in the late Victorian age: fixed-spool reels appeared before the First World War and began to approach today's level of the art in the 1950s. Indeed, the Mitchell 300 has lasted from that day to this, and there are many of us who remember the Felton Crosswind and the Ambidex range with affection. Never before though, has there been the staggering choice that faces today's angler.

MULTIPLIER REELS

The multiplier has been firmly established as the favourite sea reel, largely because of the use of very heavy lines in that branch of the sport. Multipliers also have a place in freshwater fishing when the going is particularly rugged. However, many freshwater anglers have been brought up with the fixed-spool reel only and it goes against the grain to consider using the multiplier reel.

In this piece, Gord Burton looks at the pros and cons of the multiplier reel and comes down very firmly in favour of it. Having used both types of reel extensively, I would not disagree with much of what he has got to say, although I would add that when trolling,

Gord is in no doubt that multipliers do the business!

the modern baitrunners are a tremendous advantage. The baitrunner system is set so precisely that it gives line to the gentlest of takes. However, that is my only reservation with what Gord has to say: when the lines are 15lb or less, I am happy to use a large baitrunner when trolling rather than a multiplier– but that again is a personal choice. Read on and I think that you'll be convinced . . .

'It's over ten years now since a debate has featured in the angling press concerning the use of multiplier reels for pike fishing. While some specialist pikers extolled the virtues of using this type of reel, myself included, there were others who couldn't see the advantages of using one or couldn't come to terms with using them at all. Specialist pikers, such as

Andy Harker, Alan Beat, Neville Fickling and I, penned full-length features dealing with the pros and cons of using multipliers and fixed-spool reels for piking.

At that time there were very few anglers who did, in fact, use multiplier reels, and with the exception of a small number of lure fishing enthusiasts using this type of reel and crank-handled bait-casting rods, the only reference to piking with multipliers was in the writings of the late Dick Walker on fishing Loch Lomond. Dick strongly advocated the use of heavy lines, powerful rods and multipliers for tackling these legendary fighting pike, and I was one who quickly heeded this advice; and in all my writings on lure fishing, trolling and big water piking, I have always advised multipliers as my top choice of reel.

On big waters like Ireland's Mask, the multiplier comes into its own.

In recent years I have noted an upsurge in the popularity of multipliers, especially among anglers fishing big lochs regularly, and also at the lure championships at Thorpe Park.

Many anglers approach me with queries regarding using a multiplier and it is surprising just how many mistakenly think there is one great difficulty in using them, and are afraid of the 'bird's nest' syndrome long associated with the casting of this type of reel. However, if the angler uses the drag system correctly, there is no need whatsoever to worry about tangling over-runs. I regularly play fish into the darkness during the summer months and still cast accurately into pockets and holes in reeds and weedbeds without fear of tangles.

Recommended Models

I have been using multipliers for various branches of piking for many years: the Abu range 5000 and 6000 series for most aspects of fishing with the 9000 for trolling with lead-cored lines. The Ryobi T-1 and T-2 are also great reels that hold their place in my collection. I have fished extensively, and I mean extensively, with a multiplier for plug fishing since winning a 5001C from *Angler's Mail* back in 1973, and in actual fact some of my reels are made up of replacement spares as I gradually wore a reel out! There is no better reel for trolling, plug fishing or boat fishing and I cannot praise it too highly.

Amongst the plus points in favour of a multiplier is that it functions well when loaded with heavy lines. When fishing afloat on the big lochs I generally use lines of 17lb–18lb test because more often than not I am fishing in rugged conditions and some of my plug-fishing sessions are for long periods. This heavier test line helps combat the stress of continual casting.

Casting Benefits

Owing to the fact that line leaves the multiplier directly from the spool there is little resistance, but there is a build up of friction when the line peels from the spool of the fixed-spool reel, and in heavy lines this severely restricts the distance one can cast, especially when fishing with small-sized plugs. This doesn't happen when using the multiplier set-up, and I can make lengthy casts when using plugs as light as ⅝oz.

I'll refer to a session I had with Dave Phillips on Tullyguide Lake in Ireland; he was using an 11ft rod and fixed-spool reel loaded with 18lb line, but I was out-casting him using a 6¾ft single-handed bait-casting rod armed with a multiplier loaded with 17lb Platil. When fishing alongside Des Taylor at Thorpe Park, I was casting just as far as he was while using the same set-up. Another plus point in favour of a multiplier, especially so when plug fishing, is that the line lay on the spool is always even, whereas on a fixed-spool reel it can often be loose and uneven. To keep the line lay even on the fixed-spool reel, the line must be retrieved taut at all times, but this cannot be done if you're working the plug in a slow spasmodic fashion, but the multiplier retrieves the line evenly, even when retrieving loosely hanging from the rod top. The multiplier is purely and simply a superior tool for the plug fisher.

A multiplier also performs better for casting large, heavy deadbaits. There is no snatch on line when casting due to direct thumb pressure on the reel drum. When the thrust of the cast is made, it is done in one smooth motion and I can launch big whole mackerel over a hundred yards with no problems.

Clutch Benefits

The clutch system on the multiplier is another point in its favour, especially so when playing big, powerful pike right up close to the boat, but also when a big fish smashes on to a lure right at the end of the retrieve at the bankside or at the boat. Let me explain: over the years hundreds of pike have chomped their toothy jaws on to a lure in this situation, sometimes just as the plug is lifted from the water; you can actually hear the crunch of the jaws on the lure!

Now then, due to the fact that I always have the clutch set slack, the pike can easily bolt away, taking the line from the lightly set drag. Thumb pressure on the drum of the multiplier can be applied to pull the hooks home and restrain and then play the fish.

This is not the case when using a fixed-spool reel if the clutch is set tight, as it is by many anglers. When a pike bolts, the result can often be breakage because of the sudden shock of the smashing take and the fact that you cannot give line fast enough by back-winding in this situation. If the clutch on a fixed-spool reel is set slack, there will be an ear-piercing screech as the rod sweeps back and you cannot strike properly when set like this. However slack the clutch is set on the multiplier, tension can immediately be applied to the taking fish by putting that thumb pressure on the spool. There is no screaming clutch, just a restraining hold on a firmly hooked pike!

It is in the playing of big, powerful pike that multipliers show their true worth. Whilst I have caught lots of big pike from lochs using fixed-spool reels, there is no doubt in my mind that a multiplier is the superior tool for the job. Big loch pike are renowned for their fighting qualities and are the only fish I have taken that have made repeated runs of up to forty yards from the side of the boat; they are the only big pike that I have had tailwalk up to four times during their battles for freedom – wheee haaa – terrific stuff! The big 'trout stocked' water pike have never fought anything like as hard or tailwalked at all! If you are using a fixed-spool reel, long screaming runs against the clutch damages line and you cannot keep up with a big loch pike by backwinding when it bolts off on a long run. I have seen so many anglers smashed in such instances.

One very noticeable thing about hooking big pike when boat fishing is that they can be brought right up close to the boat almost like guiding a dog on a lead: that's when the fish realizes that something isn't right (it has been hooked!) and it explodes into life, lashing the water violently and bolting away, wrenching the rod round. This is how these pike gained their legendary reputations for fighting hard.

Many, many times I have had to plunge the rod down into the water when a big fish has sounded to the deeps bucking the rod hard. When a fish bolts under the boat, it is easy to disengage the reel and put it into free spool allowing the pike to keep on going, but keeping direct contact due to thumb pressure on the drums, it's so easy! Then simply take the rod around the stern and wind straight back into battle! There is no better reel for trolling because again the clutch system (Star Drag), can be adjusted just tight enough to give line when a pike chomps on to a plug, but with enough tension on the line to pull the hooks home. This cannot be done adequately if you are trolling with a fixed-spool reel due to the line kinking and twisting from a tight-set clutch.

Trolling

When trolling with natural live- and dead-baits, the free-spool system can be tightened just enough to tow the baits along, yet with a sufficiently light adjustment to allow the pike to run off freely. As for being difficult to use, it is no such thing; 'bird's nests' are only experienced by anglers who do not use the reel correctly. The reels handle all lines without difficulty, and by counting the crossings of the level wind across the spool the angler can always know how much line he has got out behind the boat when trolling.

The multiplier is a superior reel in all of the above aspects of piking, and finally, there is nothing quite as pleasing as a screaming clicker on a multiplier when a big fish has picked up a bait and gone!

Whoop and wheee haaa! You're in!'

THE CENTREPIN REEL

Like life, fishing tackle has its ups and downs and for many years, once the fixed-spool reel was perfected, few anglers were seen using the centrepin. Those that did employ the services of the centrepin were seen as eccentric or rather cultish: true, there were attempts to popularize its use in the 1970s but this was only a fringe affair. During the latter 1980s and now into the 1990s, the centrepin is back with a vengeance. More and more anglers are realizing that for a lot of river work it is absolutely unbeatable: trotting with a fixed-spool reel in many cases is a nonsense by comparison. Also, for pure aesthetics, there is little to beat playing a good fish on the centrepin. We do not fish to eat, but for enjoyment, and we might as well enhance this as much as possible. New Year 1993 saw me using my old Aerial centrepin on the River Tay for bright, spanking Scottish grayling. The whole affair was a delight – even when the float was not going down. It was a pleasure in itself to use a beautiful piece of machinery to the limit of my own abilities – however limited.

My own experiences of the centrepin are many and happy (apart from when the wind blows and I get into an infernal tangle). However, I have not made a study of them in anything like the depth that Alan Tomkins has. Here he condenses his enormous knowledge.

'For much of my fishing, where range isn't that important, and especially on rivers, I like to use centrepins, and most of the time, partly for aesthetic reasons, I choose to use the older type. The sight of an old centrepin is almost guaranteed to provoke comment from other anglers, and I'm often asked where to obtain such a reel. Unless you are very lucky (and they do still turn up in car boot sales!), it isn't that easy, and certainly not cheap to buy a really good old centrepin. However, that need not stop you owning a good centrepin of the modern variety, and the purpose of this article is to draw comparisons between the older reels and their modern counterparts. I shall be looking mainly at the reel's suitability as a trotting reel; as for legering, things aren't quite as critical. If you are casting properly, and by that I mean casting from the reel, such as in the Wallis cast, and not pulling loops of line from between the rodrings, then you will need a properly balanced reel even for legering.

Old Reels

It is obvious from bankside conversations I have had over the years that many of the anglers who question me about these old reels have never used one, or, if they have, they haven't used it properly. There are drawbacks in using the older reels, and the most common of these is that the pins which support

the line are set too far down the spool, meaning that unless you put plenty of backing on the reel, or spool on several hundred yards of line, you will have trouble retrieving line quickly. I have found neither of the above solutions practical. I have tried many different types of backing, ranging from different types of line to various kinds of sticky tape, but I always get the same problem – that of the line sticking. With the tape, the adhesive always seems to work its way on to the line, causing it to stick and leave the reel unevenly. With the backing line, the trotting line digs in and again sticks. This can be alleviated to some extent by putting the line on the reel backwards, so it comes from the top of the spool instead of the bottom. Personally, I don't like doing this as it makes Wallis casting far more difficult, if not impossible and also because I hate reeling the wrong way!

Digging in is a problem you will often get with centrepins, and it is very difficult to trot smoothly when this occurs. It can be

Note the line guard on this old Aerial.

minimized by using the least amount of line possible, and I generally spool my centrepins up with 50–70yd of line, which up to now I have found adequate. If you do require longer lengths of line on a centrepin, it is better to go for a wide drum rather than a narrow drum, as the line will be more widely spread on the spool, not overlaying itself to the same degree that it will on a narrow spool. I tend to try to do without backing, as this accentuates the digging-in problem. One thing you should be aware of in case you are tempted to put long lengths of heavy line on a centrepin, is that monofilament does contract, and the pressures exerted can be severe enough to ruin a reel completely. If for any reason, I do need backing, or in the case of reels where I need up to 100yd of heavy line, then I always use a soft line such as Dacron to back it, thereby protecting the reel from damage.

The other main drawback with some of the older reels is the line guard. If you wish to use the Wallis cast (and I recommend it) then a line guard makes this very difficult. Some of the older reels have removable line guards, but on others the guard is in the form of a cage and therefore an integral part of the reel.

Don't make the mistake of believing that all the old centrepins were good – some of them were terrible, and I honestly don't know how people fished with them – some of them would need a combination of raging flood-water and a pike bung to pull line from the reel! The old reels I would recommend are the Allcock's Aerials, particularly in the larger sizes, from 3¾in diameter upwards, and the Speedias.

Aerials come in many shapes and sizes, and in various states of wear. Look for one that spins freely, without wobbling, and without too much play on the pin. Wobbles can be got rid of by adjustment of the spokes (a bit like straightening a buckled wheel) but this can be a very frustrating exercise and unless you have a great deal of patience, I don't recommend you attempt it. Many times, after fiddling with an Aerial for hours I have almost eliminated the wobble, then in attempting to attain perfection, have tried one adjustment too many, and have had to start all over again. At times, some of my Aerials have come close to being hurled through the window!

Play on the actual pin can be taken up by adjusting the small grub screw which bears down on the pin, but don't tighten it right down – there should be a fractional amount of play there or the reel will not spin as freely as it may do otherwise. Top the pin with a small drop of oil. The oil Abu used to supply with their multipliers was excellent though I don't know if you can buy it separately. If you are fortunate enough to find a reel that has had hardly any use, then it may need running in. To accelerate this process I used to put little paper 'sails' into the holes in the drum, then let it spin for days in front of a hair-dryer, or small fan heater. The Aerial I most frequently use is a 4in wide drum model, made in approximately 1930. The only drawback with the older Aerials is that most of them seem to have been made for anglers who wind in with their right hand. While this has little effect on a reel without a line guard, it does mean that the ratchet is the wrong way round, and is far noisier when reeling in than when paying out line. Some of these can be adjusted by moving the ratchet 'peg' or bending the spring which holds it in place, but on others you will be stuck with a very noisy ratchet when reeling in.

Speedia An excellent trotting reel, which comes with either a wide or narrow drum. It is a reel I use extensively for trotting and it casts beautifully. Its only drawback is that the line pins are set too far down the spool, and you may need to use backing. I'm at a loss to

A good centrepin will spin and spin and spin ....

as good as a good Aerial or Speedia for trotting and casting. The Silex was designed as a spinning reel for casting heavy baits, so does not come into the category anyway.

Before leaving the older reel, I shall mention one thing about the method of retrieving line. Many anglers do this by continually 'batting' the spool on the side and, to facilitate this, some anglers even remove the handle from their reels; indeed, much to my regret one of the prettiest and most free-running Aerials that I own has had the handles sawn off by some Philistine! By retrieving line in this manner you are putting pressures on the pin and bearing that they were never meant to cope with, and this will eventually affect the reel. It is far better to retrieve by giving the reel a good spin from the handles, or by gently batting the bottom of the drum.

Modern Reels

I have experience of three of the more modern reels, and though there are other good modern centrepins around, I cannot describe them all, so I have chosen the ones I have experience of, and which I consider to be a good representative selection. These are the Adcock Stanton, the Dave Swallow centrepin and the Trotting Special made by Specialist Tackle, who also market an extensive range of copies of older reels. I will take them in the order I have mentioned them, and first describe the Adcock Stanton.

Adcock Stanton This is a beautifully made and very attractive reel, and terrific value for money. It runs on ball races, and is one of the freest-running centrepins I have seen. For those used to reels that run on a pin, the slight churning noise from the bearings may initially be somewhat disconcerting. However, that won't worry you for long – this reel just spins and spins, and I believe you could almost trot

understand why a reel intended primarily for fish such as roach, dace and chub should have a line capacity of about 400yd of 3lb line! I suppose if you could bear to do it, then you could have an extra set of pins fitted above the existing ones. However, my Speedias are in mint condition, and I don't fancy having them hacked about! The Speedia doesn't have the spokes as the Aerial does, so you are less likely to find them out of balance. Whilst they are not as aesthetically pleasing to look at as an Aerial, they are every bit as good to fish with, and if you can find one, they are generally cheaper than the Aerials (at least they were before this article was published!).

I have used other well-known centrepins, such as the Trudex, Rapidex, Silex and Flick 'em. I know I shall upset some people who swear by these reels by saying it, but I find neither the Rapidex, Trudex or the Flick 'em anything like a feather down a stillwater on it! The line pins are set well up the reel, giving a good rate of line retrieve, and one good flick of the spool will bring most of the line back to you on a medium trot. So having sung its praises both aesthetically, and as a trotting reel, are there any drawbacks? The most obvious, which probably won't worry too many people, is that it is not a particularly good Wallis casting reel. Not that you can't perform the Wallis cast with it; you can, but you may not cast as far as you could with something like a Speedia.

The Adcock Stanton comes with (or without) a ratchet, and though this is a little noisy on the model I have, and is rather fiddly to engage as it cannot be reached by a hand holding the rod, it does work. I would recommend you have the ratchet model as, once run in, the reel is so free-running that if you put it down for a moment it starts spinning by itself! And of course, it isn't really a practical proposition to leger using a free-running centrepin that has neither a ratchet nor a drag, unless you hold the rod all the time. I believe Cliff Adcock has improved the ratchet further since I received my reel, and that you now have the option of having a drag fitted. You can buy the reel with or without handles, though I prefer to have handles on mine as I tend to use them for bigger fish, such as barbel. I shouldn't wish to be retrieving by means of a finger in the hole in the pool when a good barbel takes off! The reel has a serrated rim to facilitate finger braking of the drum, especially when it is set. I must admit this has never caused me a problem, but it may depend on which finger you use to brake – many people use their little finger, but I tend to use my ring finger and find this more comfortable. The only criticism I would offer here, and it again relates to Wallis casting where you need to brake a rapidly spinning pool, is that the inner edge of the rim is a little square, and would be more comfortable

if it was slightly rounded off, and perhaps if the knurling was more lightly etched.

Once you have the float in the water this is a superb trotting reel, and I would definitely recommend it, especially if you are fishing waters with little flow. As well as the natural aluminium finish, which is really very attractive (unless the fish see it!), it also comes in black, and is available in three different sizes 4in, 4½in and 5in, all with a wide drum. The reel is available from tackle shops, or you can telephone Cliff Adcock on 0602 255963.

Dave Swallow I have used this centrepin only recently. It has not got quite the aesthetic appeal of the Adcock Stanton – though this is a personal thing – but in all other respects it is an excellent reel, both for casting and trotting. It comes as one basic model, with several slight variations. There is the match version, with drag but no ratchet. The specialist version is the opposite, with ratchet and no drag, though you can have both if you wish. The ratchet lever is similar to that on the Speedia, and conveniently situated in a position where it may be engaged easily with the hand holding the rod. The reel I have is meant for anglers who wind in with their left hand, and the ratchet lever is positioned accordingly. It is set to be quieter when reeling in than when giving line. The reel can be supplied with or without handles and the lightly knurled rim is standard, though you may have an unknurled rim if you wish. The inner edge of the rim is slightly rounded, making finger braking on the Wallis cast quite comfortable.

This reel also runs on ball races, and as with most centrepins, will benefit from a period of running in. Again the line supports are high in the spool, eliminating the need for backing, and giving a good retrieve rate. For a small extra charge you can have a line guard fitted, and if you don't intend to use the Wallis cast,

I would recommend you do this. You can always take it off again. An advantage with this reel is that you can have it supplied with spare spools, enabling you to carry lines of different breaking strains and the spool is easily changed by undoing the large brass nut on the back of the reel.

With its easily accessible and sweet-sounding ratchet, I would recommend this reel to the specimen hunter who wishes to use a centrepin for both trotting and legering. The Swallow centrepin is in a permanent state of evolution, so if you are interested in buying one, it may be as well to ring Dave Swallow and check on the latest developments first.

It is available in tackle shops as well as from Dave Swallow himself. For further information ring him on 0425 473658.

Specialist Tackle of Essex This range includes copies of the famous Match Aerial, which come in both narrow and wide drum, the older wide-drum Aerials and the smaller 3¾in diameter wide-drum Aerial. They also make copies of the Trudex and Flick 'em though I understand that the Trudex and Flick 'em are being discontinued, so if you want one of these, phone them up quickly! There are also plans to make a 4½in Rapidex. The latest addition to the range is the Speedia. This is one of the favourite reels, so I will be interested to see one. All of these reels are exact copies of the originals, and all have ratchets and tension adjusters.

Top of the range is the Trotting Special, which is the model I have. This reel also runs on ball races, and every single part of it is hand-made. It comes with either a wide or narrow drum, and looks to be loosely designed on the Match Aerial. Mine is black, though I understand you can have virtually any colour you wish. It spins very well straight from the box, though undoubtedly this will improve even further after a period of running

in. The ratchet is similar to the one fitted to the later Match Aerials, operated by turning knob situated on the back plate. This can be engaged by the hand holding the rod, though it is a little difficult to do so, and I feel it would be easier to operate if the catch were in the form of a lever, as it was on the 3½in Aerial made in the 1950s, instead of the round knob, which is a rough copy of the later Match Aerials. I believe Pete Henwood is looking into the possibility of using a Speedia type ratchet on this reel, which will be even better. The ratchet sounds sweet, and the tensioner works well. The rim is unknurled and rounded, providing for comfortable braking of the spool. The spool is easily changed by releasing a small spring-loaded catch located on the front of the spool, in the same manner as the Allcocks Aerials. This mechanism is little stiff on my reel, though I imagine it will loosen up with more use. As a trotting reel can't fault it. As a casting reel (Wallis), would put it on par with the Adcock Stanton that is reasonably good, but not quite as good as the Swallow. They are available in tackle shops, and for more details phone Pete Henwood on 0708 730513.

Summary

To sum up the modern reels then, all of them have the advantage of having the line supporting pins set well up on the spool something which many older reels do not have, and which I consider to be a serious drawback. They all spin very well after a running-in period, and more importantly, the are all available. They are all very well made indeed, and to be honest there is little to choose between them, and in the end it will probably come down to personal preference. Aesthetically, I think the Adcock has the edge, while for Wallis casting the Swallow is just in front. I prefer to ratchet on the

Swallow reel, but like the line tensioner on the Trotting Special. I also prefer the method of removing the spool on the Trotting Special, which is the same as on the Aerials, though this has to be a minor consideration. Which one do I use? Well, I shall use all three, probably the Adcock and the Trotting Special for roach and dace, and the Swallow for chub and barbel. I still prefer my older centrepins, but if you can't find a good one of these, then I would recommend you look at these three reels, which in practical terms are every bit as good as most of the older models. And if you still hanker after an old reel, then why not give Pete Henwood a ring and get him to make a copy for you.

If this does get you into centrepins, then you may find you need more than one to carry lines of different breaking strains, so why not buy one of each?'

FIXED-SPOOL REELS

Early models of this now all-conquering pattern began to appear in late Victorian England, but it was the Illingworth model designed in 1905 that is the true forerunner of the reels we use today. Of course, the Illingworth reel never received wide acclaim while silk lines were in general use, but from the 1940s with the advent of nylon, the fixed-spool concept increasingly caught on. What is fascinating is that the fixed-spool reel initially was heavily criticized. To many, it was seen as a way of cheating: casts could be incredibly (for the day) long and easily made. A myth grew that the reel would only work with the finest line and so the bigger fish would break away and perhaps even die with the lure in their mouths. In the 1950s the fallacy also existed that any angler should learn to cast with a centrepin before graduating to the fixed-spool reel. All of this was traditionalist

nonsense and fortunately today it has all been disproved.

Many of the fixed-spool reels of the immediate post-war era were classics. The fabulous Mitchell 300, the Ambidex and the Felton Crosswind all set remarkably high standards and it is not unusual to see models in use to this day – in fact, the Mitchell 300 still keeps going from decade to decade and never looks like dying.

In any well-stocked tackle shop today, the angler will be faced with a bewildering choice of fixed-spool reels. Many companies make them and every company has many models and the array of choice is quite staggering. There are, however, some guidelines. Most obviously, the angler tends to get what he pays for. This blinding truth is applicable to life as well as fishing, but it does hold true. Many of the cheaper reels are quite satisfactory but you must not expect from them years of total reliability in the most

Mitchells stand up to any abuse.

The Mitchell 300 range is still going strong.

rugged conditions. Having said the obvious, we can move to another blinding revelation: choose your reel to match your fishing! By that, I mean it is absurd to buy the biggest fixed-spool reel you can find if your fishing is going to be for gudgeon or skimmer bream on a canal. Equally, if your target is big carp or pike then it is ridiculous to buy a tiny fixed-spool reel that can only hold 50yd of 10lb line. Of course, many reels offer a compromise and can be used for most styles of fishing. This was the beauty of the Mitchell 300: it would cope happily with record-sized carp and still perform adequately for 4oz roach. There are many modern, medium-sized fixed-spool reels that fit this very adaptable role. Ideally, the all-round fixed-spool reel will offer different spools that might take 100yd of 3lb line and, say, 180yd of 10lb line. If you are absolutely sure that your fishing is for smaller species then by all means go for the light, shallow spool fixed-spool reel; by the same logic, if all you are interested in is monsters, then spend your hard-earned money on

the big, serious-capacity fixed-spool reels available today.

Another decision that has to be made is whether to go for a closed-faced reel or the more usual open-faced reel. This dilemma is quite easily dealt with. The closed-faced fixed-spool reel is primarily used with very light lines when fishing a stick float close in to the bank. This is not a casting reel par excellence, nor does it operate well with lines much over 3- or 4lb breaking strain. A closed-faced reel is the tool for the matchman for it is light, delicate and speedy. Its applications, therefore, are limited but it is an excellent tool for the jobs for which it was designed.

Apart from cost and size, there are many other things to look for when buying the traditional, open-faced, fixed-spool reel. One of the more important is the gearing. The criteria are that the gears should be strong, have a good cut to their teeth and mesh well with the corresponding gear. There is nothing worse than winding the handle and feeling the gears inside the body beginning to grind and to slip. This is happening now on one of my old Mitchell 300s: I cannot blame the reel, for it has given me sterling service over at least twenty years, so it is probably time to retire it. However, I have bought one or two modern reels and found that the gearing has begun to slip after only a few months of work. The gearing is especially important if you are asking the reel to do a lot of hard work, for example, to play heavy fish in tight situations or spend its life reeling in heavy swimfeeders against strong currents. The lighter the work, the less the load on the gearing.

A vital consideration is the drag mechanism. Obviously, when a fish pulls over a certain preset limit, the spool should turn and give line to avoid breakage. This is one of the great benefits of the fixed-spool reel: in theory, the fish should never be allowed to break the line. In practice, this does happen all too often. Many drag systems are not smooth and tend to snatch. Try the tension out very, very carefully in the tackle shop. The same amount of pull on the line should start the spool moving again and again. A poor drag system needs much more pull on the line to make it move initially than it would subsequently need in order to control the run of the fish. Everything must be smooth and controlled with wide variation and adjustment. It is important that adjustments can be made quickly and easily during a battle, so ensure that the controls are not tight or finicky.

Indeed, it has been the unreliability of drag systems over the years that has led to the great 'playing debate'. There are many anglers today who prefer to put the reel in to backwind and let a running fish take line in this way rather than from the spool. This method of playing fish has *only* come about because many drag systems have operated badly and inefficiently under pressure, and a big fish has not been able to take line smoothly at the start of its run. There is no intrinsic advantage in allowing the fish to take line through backwinding the reel, and in theory the traditional idea of the slipping spool is a much better way of giving line. Thankfully, there are reels on the market today that do have efficient drag systems and the days of back-winding could be on the way out. Because this is so important, I will mention the Shimano reels here: I have used their larger models for four years now and have yet to experience any problems with the drag system, even in air temperatures of well over 100°C (212°F) in Asian summers or the low freezing in our piking winters.

The body of the reel also deserves a mention. Many are too brittle, especially those made of plain carbon fibre. A brittle body will have a tendency to break, especially around the stem where it fits into the reel seat. Drop your reel on a towpath on a cold, frosty morning and that will be the end of your day's fishing. Again, it is worth mentioning that Shimano use a material known as XT7 in their bodies rather than plain carbon fibres and this, apparently, makes them much more flexible and hard wearing.

A lot of talk these days centres around the use of ball-bearings in reels. The common question is to ask how many ball-bearings the reel has, but the important points are more subtle. For example, are the ball-bearings sealed and stainless? There are many grades of ball-bearing races, and some of the cheaper ones easily rust and become absolutely useless. The more expensive the reel, the higher grade of ball-bearing race that is likely to be fitted. So remember that number is not all important but quality plays a vital role.

In the modern fishing scene there is more and more emphasis on long casting, and here the fixed-spool reel is the master. However, it is vital to investigate how the line is laid and how long and tapered the spool is. It is very important that the spools are genuinely long and are actually tapered, as there are some pseudo long spools available. These have a long appearance, if you see what I mean, but are not in fact long enough for the purposes for which they were intended. It is also important that the crosswind of the line is effective and fills the whole length of the spool. Some reels do not lay down the line properly the whole length, and this makes for bunched line and poor casting.

Any reel can go wrong, and it is important to think about the guarantee, especially as few tackle dealers nowadays are equipped for doing repairs on site. That sort of skill seemed to die some twenty or thirty years ago. We live increasingly in a world market and many reels now sold in this country were made many thousands of miles away. It is essential therefore that your guarantee is actually valid for the country you live in. You need to ensure that you get spare parts and maintenance for many years to come, and this is only likely to be available in the country in which the product was originally marketed. Do check this particular point very carefully with your tackle dealer before making any purchase.

Technology continues to advance the concept of the fixed-spool reel, and several years ago the baitrunner concept was introduced. This facility proved a godsend for carp anglers the country over, and now it is rare to see a serious carp man use any other type of reel. The baitrunner option is, however, useful for many other types of angling. For example, whilst barbelling recently, I noticed my colleague fishing a second rod with a small deadbait at the tail of the swim. He was float fishing primarily, but this bait was lying there just in case a large barbel came along. The bait, a small, dead bleak, was fished on a baitrunner reel and the mechanism was set so that the current couldn't pull off line but a taking fish would make that spool shriek. He did not get a bite on the deadbait that par-

ticular day but the method shows the versatility of the baitrunner option, and it should be taken into account when buying such an expensive piece of tackle. The baitrunner also is a valuable option for the man who does a great deal of trolling (see page 39).

Most fixed-spool reels wobble a little when they are wound in rapidly. Shimano have introduced a new concept called Dyna Balance. This relates to the balance of the moving part in the reel and is a totally new concept. The advantages of Dyna Balance are enormous but can hardly be put into words. Pick one up in a tackle shop or use one at the river bank and you will find that the 'feel' is totally different. Dyna Balance is another step towards that ultimate fixed-spool reel.

CLOSED-FACED REELS

It is time to mention the closed-face reel, which is unbeatable for very light tackle control where long casting is not very important. Casting can be done one-handed, control of the line could not be easier, and both of these factors make the closed-faced reel the perfect choice for the close-in stick float angler. Also, because the spool is covered, the line is not as susceptible to problems caused by the rain or wind. However, the closed-face reel is not generally as fast on the retrieve nor as good for long casting. Nor is it particularly rugged and up to the job of hunting big fish. The bail-arm mechanism of the open-faced reel is probably more reliable than the pick-up in the closed-face variety. Really, it is a question of horses for courses, and if most of your fishing is going to be done for decent-sized specimens at long range, opt for the open-face variety. If, however, you are concentrating on float fishing and delicate work at quite close range, a good closed-face reel is certainly something to look out for.

4 Line

The situation in nylon lines has changed rather dramatically over the last ten years or so. During the 1960s and 1970s a large number of specialist and match anglers went to great lengths to try and discover the best lines available to suit their purposes. All manner of tests were devised and Newcastle University, I think it was, even donated their scientific department to help with some of the tasks. Of course, all this was highly creditable since nothing (apart from perhaps hooks) is more important than the line that attaches angler to fish.

Most of the line available in our shops today is made in West Germany by Bayer. Any differences tend to be in marketing and

It is at moments like this that the line is given its most searching test.

packaging. Although there is some variation in the raw materials used and slightly different grades of line are produced, by and large, most brands are much the same. However, there is some room for difference in terms of density and the general make-up of the line. For example, if the line is made light it tends to float and is excellent for float fishing. On the other hand, if the line is made rather more dense it becomes at least semi-sinking and is exactly what the leger fisherman requires. Apart from these basic differences, most modern line is reasonably resistant to abrasion and fairly standard. Providing it is looked after reasonably, it should last well. The best market sellers are undoubtedly 1.7lb, 2.6lb and 3.2lb for float fishermen and 3-, 4-, 5-, 6- and 8lb for more general angling.

This just about covers monofilament line. However, there is another major type of line called copolymide, and this is generally made in Japan. The best example of a copolymide line is Double Strength, which is marketed by Drennan. During the 1970s there was an attempt to make stronger lines thinner by pre-stretching them. Platyl Strong was the notable example of this and it did serve some purpose. However, it was unpredictable and nowhere near as good as its 1990s successor. Lines like Double Strength are lower in diameter for their breaking strain than general lines. They have less stretch and are very easily damaged. If they are nicked or kinked, they become much more prone to break unexpectedly. There is one rule in using these high-tech lines: do not drop in diameter, but rather keep the same diameter and enjoy the bonus of extra strength. That said, there are times when I, at least, take a risk. For example, if I am legering in a particularly fast current then I will sometimes use Double Strength 7lb line straight through as the lower diameter is less prone to catching on the current and dislodging the feeder or the leger. However, and this is very important, I do take great care of line, and if I feel it has been damaged at all, say behind a bail arm for example, then I will change it at once.

Most copolymide lines are used for hook lengths where their lower diameter can fool a suspicious fish. However, big fish in clear water are very capable of recognizing the line well before it reaches the float or the terminal tackle. Carp and tench are just two species that can be disturbed from an area by the sight of the main line in the water, and I have found occasions where a switch to copolymide has saved the day. Copolymide lines are certainly here to stay and at the moment (in the mid 1990s) account for around 30 per cent of the market. Undoubtedly, probably before this book is published, there will be improvements in their make-up and their share of the market will rise accordingly.

It is common for different brands (often using the same line) to offer the angler a slightly different coloured line. Some anglers swear by brown, others by green, others by grey and so on. So far, however, there has been very little proof as to whether colour helps or hinders, and generally it is considered to be a matter for personal choice. However, I was once given some fluorescent yellow line which worked well in Asia in coloured water but seemed to be the kiss of death when I brought it back to troll on very clear Scottish lochs. On a couple of memorable occasions, large fish could be seen veering away from it, and certainly the rod that had standard coloured line out fished it by 10-1 over the course of three weeks. Needless to say, I got rid of that bright yellow line and have never used it again.

One of the most important things to bear in mind is that modern line is generally of a high standard, and it is important how you deal with it after purchase. Drennan, for example, lay their lines on large, wide, soft spools as this tends to give the line very little

A good fish comes to the net – now it is all down to the hook hold and the line.

memory. Too many cheap reels today offer tight, small spools which means the line is crammed on and comes off coiled, with a distinct memory. Try to buy reels with spools as wide as possible and this unfortunate characteristic of nylon line can be minimized. Also, always pay great care and attention to the last few yards of line after use – especially if you know that it has been fished close to snags or near to gravel bars. If the line feels rough or frayed then discard it, safely, at once. I stress *safely*: line is one of the greatest killers of wildlife at the waterside as it takes years to disintegrate. Never leave uncut loops of line lying around – even near the home. Always make sure that it is burned, or cut, or goes straight into a bin.

In past years, braided line has taken over the carp market – at least as far as terminal rigs go. Virtually all carp anglers use braid today, and the market leader has probably been Silkworm marketed by Kryston. Other companies like Drennan (Carp Silk) also make braids that are soft, supple and very reliable. There has been a great deal of progress made in braided lines over recent years, and different weaves produce different effects that match the various situations. Braided lines will probably soon be impregnated with carbon that will have no adverse effects on the suppleness of the material but will greatly increase the strength. For example, a carbon-impregnated braid with a diameter of 15lb line will actually have a breaking strain of 66lb! The advantages of such a break-through are obvious. Braided lines are not restricted to carp alone and have spread to other species. Unfortunately, braids and boilies have developed together, and it is important for anglers to realize that braided line can be used with all manner of baits. Braid is particularly important, I believe, in barbel fishing: wise barbel soon become accustomed to feeling the stiffer nylon with their sensitive mouths, and braided line can put the clock back many years on some waters. Braid is also more abrasion-proof than nylon line. For example, whilst preparing for a recent trip after Caspian sturgeon, I was advised by the Russians to use either 60lb nylon line or 30lb braided line. The reason was simply that the braid takes far more stick than nylon before giving way.

LINE

There are, increasingly, important specialist lines appearing on the market. Notable amongst these is Big Game, marketed by Terry Eustace. This line has won great favour among carp, pike and mahseer anglers. Indeed, compared with more usual nylon line, it is very resilient, and it will take a great deal of chafing against rocks or gravel bars before giving way. It is very expensive, but so is a trip to India or a season spent at one of our top carp lakes, and it makes no sense at all to lose the fish of a lifetime for the sake of a little extra expense. Fortunately, today, all lines are available in bulk spools. This makes life very much simpler and avoids that old nightmare of trying to calculate how much line to take off a spool before refilling it with a 100m drum. Now you can simply wind line on until the correct level is reached. Bulk spools also mean that the cost of line works out considerably cheaper.

Of course, for many types of fishing, you do not need to put on 150–200yd of new line. For example, when I am trolling, I simply spool on 70–80yd of new line for each trip. That is about as much line as I want out, and there is little chance of a fish taking line off the reel when I am in a boat. This means that I can change my line every two or three days and not find the expense too crippling.

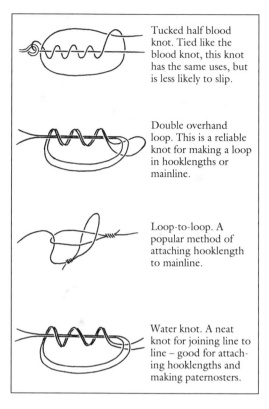

Tucked half blood knot. Tied like the blood knot, this knot has the same uses, but is less likely to slip.

Double overhand loop. This is a reliable knot for making a loop in hooklengths or mainline.

Loop-to-loop. A popular method of attaching hooklength to mainline.

Water knot. A neat knot for joining line to line – good for attaching hooklengths and making paternosters.

Useful knots.

LINES TO LOOK OUT FOR

Drennan's range of lines has a large share of the market, and they are reliable and well priced. Maxima has been very popular for many years, and is excellent for the specialist angler as it is a natural sinker. Price can be a problem. Match anglers speak very highly of Daiwa Harrier and Special Anglaise. Both these lines are excellent for stick float fishing as they are very buoyant. Specialist Anglaise is even treated with silicon which makes it probably the best floating line there is. Both have low diameters and poor memories, which means they leave the spool with no tangle-causing coils. Sylcast, Brent and Drennan have for a long time made up a large part of the specialist market which is now being threatened by the advent of Trilene – especially the Big Game brand.

5 Floats

Sadly, we are living in an age when the art of float fishing with a running line is being lost to a great degree. This is partly because so many matchmen use a pole with a fixed line and partly because so many specialist anglers are switching over to legering and swim-feeder fishing techniques. Even river anglers now often prefer to use a swimfeeder than a float and, perhaps, a bait dropper when conditions demand. This is a great shame because fishing the float brings satisfaction as well as nets full of fish. Very often, float fishing is much more productive than legering, especially for shy fish that are wary of static bait. A mobile bait can often tempt a barbel or a chub that will have nothing at all

to do with a legered bait – or at least until several hours of darkness have elapsed.

The modern float is a very precise instrument and it is mass produced, so that thousands of floats behave exactly alike. This is a far cry from the days when floats were built out of cork and quill and each one had its own characteristics. So precise is the modern float that there is little point any more in trying to make your own ... and of course, as with everything else in today's tackle market, there are innumerable choices. It is often confusing to walk into a tackle shop and see a selection of floats that seems to stretch to the horizon.

There are, however, pointers for basic starting choices. Make sure that the float you buy

A Drift Beater float accounted for this tench.

is big enough for the job. There is nothing worse than scratching around with a float which is too small either to be cast the required distance or to hold out in the current and the wind. A big float can always be overcast and drawn back into the baited area so as not to cause too much disturbance. A big float also gives you far more control than one which is too light. Today's floats are very well designed and providing you shot a big float correctly, it should be no more difficult to take under than a small one.

A basic float rule is that all stick-floats are fished top and bottom – that is, they are attached to the line in two places. These floats are perfect for close-in work, especially on rivers, but do not use them a long way out or your control over them will suffer. All other floats are really varieties of wagglers, and these should be attached to the line by their bottom end only. There are various types of attachment on the market that make swapping over a float an easy job. Failing this, you can always slide it on the line and lock it with shot.

Floats are basically either long and thin or have a certain type of body. The long, thin ones are probably the most popular, and are generally made of peacock quill – an excellent material, although sometimes reed or plastic is used. The bodies on floats are often made of polystyrene, and these can be placed down towards the bottom of the float to give greater stability in rough water. Those floats with bodies near the top are generally meant for streamy, fast water where surface stability is required.

A lot of modern floats can be rearranged, especially by using a variety of different tips which can be inserted into the top. These tips can be of different colours which will help with visibility if you change swims or as the light alters. Also, if you are having trouble registering bites, a finer insert tip can often help. Many floats are now made with clear plastic bodies, often called crystals. The idea of these is that timid fish in clear water cannot see them so easily, and are not so likely to be alarmed.

Modern floats are not cheap, so it pays to look after them well. The general run of float boxes are simply plastic tubes, and to have a lot of floats rattling around loose in these can be disastrous. It is very wise to pad both the top and the bottom with foam rubber to prevent chipping.

It would be wise now to look at the different float models on the market and examine the uses for which they were designed. Most of the names that follow are taken from the Drennan range as these are the floats most commonly found in the shops today. However, the models are often made by several companies, and overall the standard is very high. Few duff floats are made today.

Avons These are good trotting floats for quite long distances. They are perfect for chub, barbel, grayling and even large dace or roach in fairly quick water. Some Avons are made as crystals, and some are made with wire stems. The idea behind the latter modification is to give them greater stability in turbulent water. Loafer floats are rather similar and are designed for long-distance trotting and taking big lumps of bait like bread or luncheon meat long distances to chub or barbel. They are perfect in fast- or medium-paced rivers and swims where the surface boils to some extent. They are certainly visible for up to sixty yards. I have also found Loafers very useful as live- or deadbait floats for perch. I am sure they would be equally useful for zander.

Most river fishing is done with the ordinary stick float that will come in several sizes. It is important to fish these top and bottom and to string the shot down the line, shirt-button style. The smaller stick floats are designed for close-in fishing and delicate work for roach, dace, chub and barbel. Maggots, casters and hemp make perfect hookbaits. By fishing the float top and bottom, it can be held back so that the bait is moving a little slower than the current. The float can also be stopped completely, and this raises the bait somewhat in the water and often induces a bite.

There is a range of big stick floats that are also fished top and bottom and are designed to cope with faster, deeper water. These can also take bigger baits like pieces of flake, lobworm or luncheon meat. Rather similar are the double rubber bolster floats. These have a big, strong body and are designed to take a great deal of bulk shot set 12–18in from the hook. This makes them absolutely ideal for slightly faster swims and boiling water where the bait needs to get down quickly.

The Zoomer was also originally designed to be fished top and bottom, and fished on slower rivers where it could be held back as far as mid-stream. It was very popular when it was first brought out, as it is loaded in the base. This means it needs less shot on the line, which in turn means less damage to delicate hook lengths and provides for a slow-sinking bait – perfect for a wary bream shoal feeding at range on a Fenland drain.

Probably the most common floats bought today are the ordinary peacock wagglers. These are simply constructed of peacock quill and come in many different sizes. They are ideal for all general approaches in rivers and

A huge chub like this demands the most sensitive presentation.

in lakes. They are in fact the perfect waggler float, and baits can be fished on the drop by pushing the weight up towards the float. They are buoyant enough to allow a bait to be dragged through the swim without constantly registering false bites, and are also satisfactory floats for presenting a bait static at depth.

However, the basic peacock waggler is bound to have variations, and one of these is the Polywag. This has the peacock antenna but incorporates a polystyrene body. It is perfect for slow rivers or lakes, and the body simply gives it a little bit of stability. Very similar to this is the peacock swinger, which operates in exactly the same way but is slightly smaller and possesses a finer tip. This stepped-down version maintains stability but gives a little more in the way of sensitivity for shy-biting fish, especially on cold days.

Martyn Page tries to hold a float-fooled tench from the reeds.

A very popular modern float is the Loaded Crystal. This is a clear-bodied large waggler with a bomb incorporated into its base. The bomb allows the float to be cast long distances on a very straight trajectory. The clear body means that shy fish in gin waters are less likely to be alarmed by the float. However, the loaded base does drag the float deeper on entry to the water. This means that you have to be careful if the swim is shallow and a species like bream is feeding warily. It pays to overcast and draw the float carefully back into the swim. Feathering the cast also helps to reduce the speed of the float on impact.

Another outstanding float, especially for stillwaters, is the Drift Beater. Remember that no stillwaters are ever, in fact, still. The winds always set up some sub-surface currents that will drag many lesser floats out of position and make the bait behave in a totally unnatural fashion. The Drift Beater has a long antenna and a large body beneath, which keeps it stable in even fairly strong currents. There is also a highly visual sight-bob that stands out at a distance amongst waves. You fish the Drift Beater with a certain amount of lead anchored on the bottom to prevent movement, and bites often tend to be of the lift variety. This is a very forgiving float to use and it does not need extreme delicacy. It is the perfect float for medium- to long-distance fishing on lakes for bream and tench, but it is also excellent close-in on very rough, very deep conditions for all species.

The bodied crystal float is excellent for distance fishing. The body makes it very stable and gives it greater buoyancy, thereby allowing the use of more shot per length of float. The tips of these floats are interchangeable so that sensitivity and visibility can be increased if necessary. Again, they are excellent lake and river floats.

Most of the floats that we have discussed are excellent floats for bigger fish on both rivers and stillwaters but delicate canal-type floats are also heavily in demand. One of these models is the Still Water Blue. These small floats fit the canal bill perfectly, and the larger sizes can be used on bigger stillwaters. The cane antenna makes them very sensitive and helps drop bites to be picked out clearly, while the balsa body makes them stable and allows them to combat surface drift. Greys are made entirely from balsa and designed for canals, where they are perfect for spotting minute bites. They are very sensitive indeed, and one of the most popular floats around. They are fished bottom end only, which makes them perfect for windy days.

The Link Waggler is very much like a canal grey but an innovation is the link attachment on the base. This allows greater freedom in the placing of shot as locking shot is not needed at all. There is no need for weight around the float and all the shot can be bulked further down towards the hook. The bayonet system also does not damage fine lines nearly as much as shot itself.

The Canal crystal boasts interchangeable bristles that are very fine and tapered to allow perfect bite registration. These are also designed for very clear conditions and their blow-moulded bodies make them very unobtrusive.

The popular Dart has a balsa body which is loaded, and a cane tip. This allows a couple of shot around the body and either one or two dropper shot. It is perfect for close-in work

and is extremely sensitive. Again it is fished bottom only which makes it ideal for use in windy conditions.

Most of these floats can be fitted with a Night Light insert. These can be of the Beta variety which give out a glow for many years. These come in ratings of 300 or 500 micro lamberts. The 300 version is generally visible for five to ten yards, whereas the 500 version can be seen for at least twenty-five yards. They are excellent additions for night breaming or tenching, and perhaps one day the carp world will wake up to their use. The isotope Night Lights are expensive and many companies sell 12hr lights instead that work out quite cheaply if night fishing is not a regular pastime.

Many of the northern tackle shops will sell a strange, dumpy little float called the Grayling float. This has a squat, nearly round body up near the tip that keeps the float stable in the roughest water conditions – places where grayling often thrive. This float can be fished top and bottom if you want to slow the float down a bit, and even stop it to raise a bait in the water. Or it can be fished bottom only if there is a bit of a wind and you want to keep the line off the surface. All in all, they are very easy floats to fish and offer good visibility at anything up to forty yards range – an attribute which makes them perfect for long-trotting.

All of this may sound a little frightening but remember that a lot of these floats are simply variations on a theme and are only designed to offer different presentations. A selection of stick floats and peacock wagglers with perhaps a Drift Beater or two thrown in will let you fish most rivers and stillwaters in the country with some degree of efficiency. Once you have got the hang of float fishing and the taste for it, you will want to refine your methods, and you will be surprised at just how effective some of these floats are.

6 Split Shot

The recent history of anglers' split shot is a very delicate and emotive one. It was during the 1970s that problems with split shot and waterfowl, notably swans, began to be remarked upon by members of the bird fraternity. Len Baker of the Swan Rescue Centre was a pioneer in getting to grips with this problem and, whatever we may say about his methods, Mr Baker certainly got things moving for the benefit of these beautiful birds. Soon research proved fairly conclusively that the lead in anglers' split shot was causing bird deaths. Obviously, over the centuries during which anglers had been using lead split shot, aquatic conditions in this country were changing considerably. Pollution, agrochemicals, the increased use of motor boats and all manner of other changes meant that waters were not as naturally rich as they once were. Whereas, in Victorian England, say, swans could ingest a certain amount of lead split shot and remain healthy, today that is impossible for them. So, in conjunction with other destructive factors, anglers' lead shot was banned in the 1980s. This, of course, caused horrified concern. Many anglers even forecast the end of coarse fishing as we knew it. A host of firms jumped into the breach with substitutes – some useless and some frankly hilarious. All manner of crazy schemes were dreamed up and, thankfully for us, have bitten the dust.

Today, split shot is available in lead substitutes and is virtually identical to that which we used as children. The only problem with it is that frequently the lead substitute is lighter, so the shot often tends to be bulkier than before – a small price to pay for the saving in swan life and our image with the public.

It has to be said that the new shots are infinitely more expensive than the lead of the

The **Arlesey** bomb was popularized by Richard Walker in the 1950s. The shape and built-in swivel both help a long, tangle-free cast.

The **Coffin** lead, though old fashioned, is excellent for holding bottom in quick water.

The **Barrel** lead is an invaluable lead for weighing down lures or trolled deadbaits.

Types of leger weight.

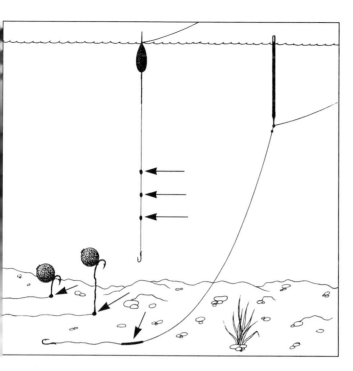

Heavy Metal applications.

past, and an attempt has been made to over-come this by offering double-cut shot that is easily re-usable. The system is ingenious and it certainly works: as one cut is squeezed tight, another one opens, and it is easy to squeeze that at the end of the day and retrieve the piece of shot from the line. The trouble is that the double-cut system does cause a number of tangles and is not particularly aerodynamic. In short, this is fine for the casual angler, but somebody more serious will go for the centre-cut shot. This sits on the line very much bet-ter, casts more accurately and presents no problems of tangling.

There are several brands of shot now on the market. Anchor Tackle make a medium-soft shot that is a pleasant grey colour but leaves its coating on the fingers. I am not convinced, either, about the efficiency of its dispensing canister. Dinsmore also make a medium-soft shot that is exactly the same size as that of Anchor Tackle. The only difference is that the

Dinsmore shot is a very shiny black colour. I am not convinced that colour makes that great a difference, but personally I prefer shot to look as unobtrusive as possible. Thamesly make a very soft shot indeed, which is possi-ble to close firmly with the fingers alone. It is a nice, dullish, coal-black colour and each one is beautifully split.

Whilst discussing split shot, it is well worth mentioning Heavy Metal, which is made and marketed by Kryston. This is the heaviest putty made to date and is as heavy as lead. The concept is easy: you simply mould it on to the line with your fingers in any shape or size that you want and then immerse it in water for 45 seconds to let it cure and harden.

There are several important considerations with Heavy Metal. Firstly, it is much kinder to the line than split shot. It does not bruise or nip it in any way; a property that is very use-ful when fine lines are being used. Moreover, Heavy Metal is much easier to slide up and down the line than split shot: simply warm it up in your fingers and you can move it about as much as you like.

For legering, Heavy Metal is excellent as you can put as little or as much on the line as you need. The weight load can be very, very precise and you are not tied to the normal increments of shop-bought leger weights. Also, if the current speeds up slightly, you can put a little more Heavy Metal on to compensate: if the flow drops away, it is easy just to nip away a piece of Heavy Metal so the lead is once again perfectly balanced. Heavy Metal is particularly good for the angler who wants to trundle his bait around the swim and needs a leger that is absolutely precise in weight.

It is, perhaps, in float fishing that Heavy Metal really comes into its own. Remember, shot is round because that is the simplest

shape to make it. If it were possible, shot would be streamlined. So, the BB equivalent in Heavy Metal can be put on to the line almost as thinly as a coat of paint and be totally cylindrical, around four or five inches long. In the water, shot drop in a vertical plane but Heavy Metal strung out thinly along the line will fall in a graceful arc and not disturb the fish in the least.

Heavy Metal is environmentally friendly, very long lasting and completely re-usable. At the end of the day, simply warm it with your fingers, strip it from the line and replace it in a box.

That is enough on shot – though it is an important item, and absolutely vital for the keen float angler. If you are inching a perfectly shotted stick float through a deep swim, you really need to get everything right.

7 Carp Tackle

It was the carp, probably the most wary of all freshwater species, that prompted the first real, modern tackle developments. All right, a 26lb carp could be caught from Mapperley Reservoir in Derbyshire in the 1930s on

Bernard Venables was one of the Carp Catchers' Club – a group that did so much for the development of carp fishing tackle.

roach tackle, but even its captor probably knew that such an event was a fluke. By and large, carp swam pretty much unmolested in British waters until the end of the Second World War and the formation of the Carp Catchers' Club. For younger readers, a dip into *Drop Me A Line* by Richard Walker and Maurice Ingham is a real eye-opener: between them, Ingham the diligent pupil and Walker the wise, searching master, investigated most items of carp tackle and discussed the building from scratch of rods, landing nets and bite alarms. You realize that only forty years ago there was no specialist carp tackle whatsoever on the market and today's bulging shelf would have absolutely staggered the angler of thirty or forty years ago. The pace hotted up considerably in the 1960s and 1970s, with many specialist carp rods appearing but even so, the real lift-off in the carp world was only seen around the beginning of the 1980s. Since then, of course, carp have become the biggest business in freshwater angling.

Once again, to the beginner especially, the problem of where to start is a serious one. There are scores of different companies competing for hard-earned money and the choice now offered is bewildering. It was almost a simpler world when you had to go out and build your own.

There is little doubt that Julian Cundiff is one of the most respected carp anglers of the modern day, and here he gives his guide to the carp tackle that he, personally, would advise.

RODS

'No one rod will cover all eventualities in carp fishing and the beginner will be looking for a pair of rods that will adapt to most carp fishing situations he is likely to meet in his first years. Though it would be nice to talk about separate rods for long distance, short distance and stalking, budget must prevail and the beginner should keep to a rod that is medium action and between 1½–2lb test curve.

As for material, a good-quality carbon rod is three or four times the cost of its fibre-glass counterpart so the angler of limited budget might restrict himself to a fibre-glass model. This will not be as light as a carbon rod, but it will do a great deal that the beginner will require of it. The glass rod might not cast quite as far and might not possess the feel of carbon, but the job will still be done. Generally speaking, any carp rod should not really be less than ten feet nor more than twelve feet. A rod of around eleven feet is a good initial choice.

In basic terms, there are three basic rod actions. Firstly there is through action, where the rod bends from the tip to the butt. The second action is a medium one where the bend is from the tip to the mid-section and third is fast action, where all the action is contained in the rod tip. Medium-action rods are probably best for the beginner.

The test curve is the amount of force required to pull the tip to a ninety degree angle to the butt. Some people believe wrongly that test curve is related to casting ability. This is not so, and casting is determined by the action of the rod and the material used as well as the weight of the lead.

The rod hoops over, the net is ready and the carp is on its side.

Big fish like this demand the best tackle.

A classic shot of the carp fisher's rods by the carp fisher's lake.

Generally a rod with a test curve of around 2lb will cover most eventualities and be able to cast a bait some seventy yards or so.

It is wise to pay attention to reel fittings and choose a rod which has a screw winch fitting. It is very embarrassing if you find that your reel is coming loose when you are playing a particularly big fish. Ensure that the fitting does keep the reel close and secure on the handle. Do not bother to keep the reel on with tape.

Most of the modern rodrings are quite satisfactory, but do make sure that the rings are nicely in line, and are not bent but are nice and smooth. Whippings should also be secure as one that comes loose could wrap itself round the main line on the cast or even worse if you are playing a fish.

A rod like this should meet most situations, and recommended rods would be the North Western SS5, the North Western SS6, and the North Western SS6A. If you can afford it, any carbon rod of medium action with a test curve of around 2lb would be excellent – but try and buy one from one of the larger, more respected companies. Of course, it is excellent if you can afford to go to one of the specialists who offer really first-class goods.

REELS

Reels present a baffling choice as there are a hundred and one models on the market. Generally, most medium size reels will suffice for basic carp fishing, and providing they meet certain specifications most manufacturers offer something suitable. The spool should be able to accommodate at least two hundred yards of 11lb line, and preferably more. Capacity will be on the outside of the spool or on the manufacturer's instruction leaflet. It is very important that you have enough line on the reel. Spare spools are also vital and you should have spools holding 8-, 11- and 15lb line so that you can alternate them to meet the demands of your swim.

The clutch is also an essential item, especially if you like to play a fish from it. It must work smoothly, because a clutch that gives off line in fits and starts is simply not good enough and will cost you fish. If your clutch does not work smoothly, you will have to play the carp by back-winding.

The bail arm should close smoothly and positively. If you have to push the bail arm over by hand, the reel is not the correct type for carp fishing. This is typical of all the quality points you should look for: reel handles should tighten up securely and spools should turn smoothly. The anti-reverse lever should engage without any need to resort to force. Recommended reels are Mitchell 300s, 410s and 810s. The Abu range is excellent and all medium size Shimano reels are perfect carp fisherman's tools.

LINE

Along with your hook, the main line between angler and fish is probably the single most important item, and needs careful choice. I am not going to take you through all the pros and cons of every available line, but I will describe two brands that I have found reliable over the years – Sylcast and Maxima. Line strengths should be a very minimum of 6lb to around 10lb as an average. Maxima has the edge over Sylcast in its suppleness and retention of a high wet-knot strength. Above 10lb Sylcast seems to come into its own. Sylcast Sorrel is the brand to buy, not the Sylcast Black which has nowhere near the long life of Sorrel.

Whatever make of line you choose, always check the line by hand as you wind in and cast

out. At the end of every session discard the last 10ft or so – very carefully. It is this part of the line which will have received most of the wear and tear, and it could be well down in strength. Water, sunlight and abrasion all eat away at the strength of your line, so beware.

The best way to purchase line today is on a bulk spool of anything up to a thousand yards. This is the most economical way of buying line, but do take a good look at it before purchase. Is it the strength and make you want? Is it covered in dust? If so, it could be old and tired, so make sure it is relatively new stock.

Recommended strengths of line for open-water surface fishing would be 8lb Maxima. For snaggy surface fishing choose 11–15lb Sylcast. For open-water legering, choose either brand between 8lb or 11lb. For fishing in dense snags, little can beat 15lb Sylcast.

Braided lines now are the common hook length between swivel and hook. Braided line

Carp gear is one of any tackle shop's best sellers.

This perch was caught on a livebait under a loafer float.

Two drifter floats bob on the horizon.

A spinner-caught pike on the bank.

A summer barbel glows in
the sunshine.

Travelling light and greeting an Indian dawn.

Two heavily kitted-out anglers
prepare for a tench session.

An eel like this
one, caught by the
late John Sidley,
tests rod, line and
hook to the limit.

A big char caught deep down in a Scottish loch. Notice the downrigger on the side of the boat and American rod-rest in the bottom corner of the photograph.

There are times when a landing net is noticeable by its absence!

A fast, streamy piece of river – ideal for the quiver-tip rod or even for touch legering.

Fish like this test tackle to the limit.

This superb carp was landed on one of the new copolymer lines.

A lovely looking float-caught pike.

is far more soft and supple than nylon, and so is more likely to allow a bait to be sucked in without suspicion. By using soft dacron, the baited hook will behave more naturally. You can test this for yourself in a bowl of water by swirling your fingers around a dacron hook length. You will see it rise and flutter in the water, whereas nylon will behave totally differently. There are now several brands of dacron on the market and you need to look for strength, suppleness and reliability. My own personal preference is for Masterbraid, which is available in strength from 1–20lb and is usually in black. A spool of a hundred yards will last you a season. Like nylon, dacron does lose its strength, and it certainly pays to put on a new length after each fishing session. For open-water legering, 8lb or 12lb dacron will suffice, but when fishing snags move up to 15- or even 20lb breaking strain.

HOOKS

This is a tricky issue because adverts, friends and gimmicks all influence hook choice. Simply put, the hook must be sharp enough to penetrate the carp's mouth tissue and strong enough to land the fish once this has happened. With all the hook sharpeners and chemically sharpened hooks now available, you have no excuse for using a blunt hook. Most carp hooks are strong enough for general fishing, and it is only when putting a bait close to snags that you need worry for the really super-strong varieties.

Recommended brands are Drennan Super Specialists, Mustad O'Shaughnessey and, for open-water surface fishing, Drennan Super Specialists sizes 8 or 10. If you are fishing near snags, the Drennan or the Mustad in sizes 4 or 6 are probably what you will need. However, there is an increasing number of new hook brands appearing on the market and many of

these are excellent in every way. Whichever brand you choose, check the hook carefully to make sure that it has been correctly manufactured. Look carefully to see that the eye has been closed properly and that the barb is neither too big nor too small. If in any doubt, throw away any hook that you think might be defective.

SWIVELS

A swivel is used to stop the lead sliding down the hook length to the hook. Leger stops are not as good for this, and tend to move and crease the line – which means a weakened line. Choose the best quality swivels that you can afford, and in preference always buy barrel swivels. To incorporate your running lead on the main line you should use a swivel with a clip on it. These are known as Italian Link Swivels, and they allow you to vary leger weights without having to keep breaking down the tackle. Berkly Swivels are excellent in sizes 4 to 10 but Mustad also make very strong items as well. Again, whichever brand you use, make sure that the swivel does move freely, and that it is not bent or weakened in any way.

BEADS

You must prevent your lead damaging the swivel knot, and a bead will help in this. You should use a bead between swivel and lead that is large enough to rest over the knot but not so big that it jams. Beads should also be used between the lead and stopknot for bolt rig set-ups. Beads are made from plastic and therefore can be worn, chipped and dangerous to the line. They are cheap, and you should get a number of different sizes and swap them regularly.

LEADS

Leads are vital casting aids, and it is wise to start with half a dozen of ½oz leads, 1oz, 1½, 2oz and 2½ leads. The most common leads are the Arlesey Bombs but Zipp Leads and Kevin Nash Cruise Leads are just two of the more modern alternatives. Whichever leads you purchase, make sure that the swivels in the top do work. If the swivel is bent or locked tangles can be caused. Whilst matt leads can be bought, most are shiny in general finish. To deaden the colour, paint them black or soak them overnight in vinegar. If you follow the latter course, make sure you wash them off thoroughly because I don't think that vinegar is a good carp attractor!

ANTI-TANGLE TUBING

Because dacron is so soft it often wraps around the main line. Such a tangle will prevent good bait presentation and could also lose a fish. To avoid this, some form of anti-tangle tubing should be used. This forms a sheath-type arrangement on the main line, and you will find that the dacron falls off the tubing rather than twisting around ordinary line. Tubing can be soft or rigid and the one rule to follow is that the hook length must be three inches or so shorter than the length of tubing, which should be stiff. Slide the tubing on to the main line before you tie on the swivel. It will then rest on the main line. Hard plastic can be threaded by simply pushing the line up the tube, but soft plastic is a little more tricky. To thread your line up soft tubing, tie your main line to a piece of wire trace. Push that up the tube – it will go through because it is rigid. When your main line appears, pull the trace wire off and tie the main line to the swivel. There are many excellent recommended tubing makes now, and the choice really is not too critical.

LANDING NETS

It is essential that you possess a landing net which will enable you to net any carp that comes along. The smallest size you should select is a net with 32in arms. A 42in armed net is even better. Make sure that the bottom of the net is stitched up properly and strongly as the last thing you want is the carp falling through the bottom. Make sure the net is deep enough to stop the carp leaping free at

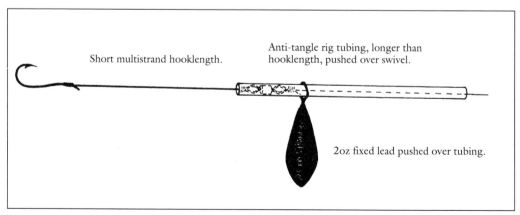

Short multistrand hooklength.

Anti-tangle rig tubing, longer than hooklength, pushed over swivel.

2oz fixed lead pushed over tubing.

Anti-tangle rig.

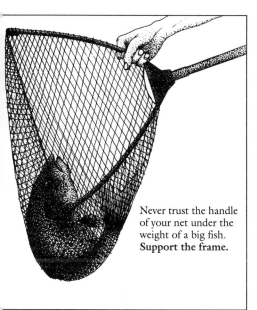

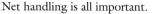

Never trust the handle of your net under the weight of a big fish. **Support the frame.**

Net handling is all important.

the end. Do not use a pole less than 5ft, and a 6ft pole could one day prove a blessing over marginal rushes. Gardener, North Western and Alan Brown all make excellent nets.

BUZZERS

Unless you are only fishing short sessions it is generally accepted that the audible bite indicator is an essential part of the carp fisherman's kit. Optonics are still probably the best indicators, but they are not cheap, and a pair represents a considerable outlay. The idea behind the optonic is that the line rests over a wheel contained in the head. Pressure on the wheel backwards or forwards turns it to break a beam of light. Each time this is broken the indicator beeps and a light on the head comes on – you have got a run. The faster the run, the closer together the beeps sound.

These are expensive items of tackle, so look after them and always make sure that the bat-

Walker, the inventive genius, with the Heron bite alarm he developed to alert a generation of carp fishermen.

teries are up to scratch. Normally the buzzers are waterproof but a smear of petroleum jelly or line grease around the seams will definitely keep any moisture out. Every so often, take the buzzer apart and clean out any moisture or dirt.

The buzzer market is increasingly big business, and every season sees new products on the market. If you cannot quite afford the optonics, have a good look around as there are some good alternatives available.

INDICATOR NEEDLES AND BOBBINS

If you intend to leger for carp – probably the most popular way of fishing – you will need a visual indicator as well as an audible one. This should be placed between the buzzer and the reel to indicate the type of take the carp is giving.

An early version of the Heron in use at Redmire.

A bobbin is a weighted item into which has been inserted a hair-type grip. This grip is then clipped on to your main line between reel and the first butt ring and pulled down to hang a few inches below the rod. Any fish moving off with the bait will move the bobbin upwards, and a fish moving towards you will cause it to fall back. These are cheap items and should be secured by a terylene tie to the front or rear rod rest. You can glue an isotope into the bobbin so that it is visible in the darkness. When you strike, the idea is that the line comes out of the hair grip and the bobbin falls to the ground. The problem is that any wind or drag will cause the bobbin to sway about or creep upwards, and this is to some extent avoided by needles and monkey climbers.

The monkey climber is rather like the bobbin inserted on to a knitting needle. The line is placed in the hole in the monkey, which is placed on the needle. In just the same way as a bobbin, a take is indicated by the climber falling or rising but it is not so affected by wind or drag. Today there is a bewildering variety of monkeys on the market and you should choose the colour and design that suits you best. Needles come in varying lengths, but one of about 24in will allow you to position the rods high off the ground. If you want your rods set low, simply push the needle deeper into the soil. Many recommendations

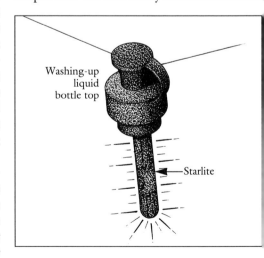

Washing-up liquid bottle top

Starlite

A glowing bobbin.

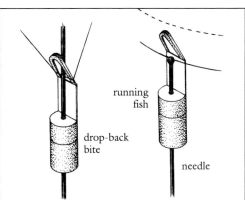

running fish

drop-back bite

needle

Pass line between the loop of the monkey climber and the needle. If possible, use a baitrunner style reel or disengage the bail arm so that the fish is free to take line.

Using the monkey.

are possible, and Gardener Tackle certainly make excellent needles, but the angling press is full of new arrivals each season, so it pays to keep your eyes open.

BUZZER BARS

Audible bite indicators need to be mounted on bars. Buzzer bars have been designed to take both optonics and rear rod-rest heads. These bars are available for both two or three rod set-ups, and the choice is really rather up to you. Remember that some fishery rules restrict you to two rods, so think carefully before purchase. Make sure that the buzzer bars have non-slip rear heads because nothing is worse than having your rod slipping down the rests when angled upwards or downwards. Take care to keep the threads of buzzer bars free from dirt and grit, and make sure that the buzzer bars are strong and well engineered without any protruding jagged bits of metal. All Gardener buzzer bars are excellently made.

BANK STICKS

You will need a pair of bank sticks, and on to these you can screw your buzzer bars to accommodate two or three rods at a time. Bank sticks have standardized threads which allow you to screw into them rod-rest heads, buzzer bars, sack clips and camera attachments. Most have an adjustable inner which allows you to vary the height at which you can set your rods. Try to purchase two pairs of bank sticks, and use one for your rods and the other two to accommodate sack clips and cameras for self-portraits. Both Gardener and Kevin Nash make excellent bank sticks. Many are made out of aluminum, and as this is a fairly soft metal you have to be careful when pushing them into stony ground. Stainless steel bank sticks will take much more abuse but they cost two or three times more than the aluminium.

CATAPULTS

Both boiled baits, surface baits and even particles often need to be catapulted into position some way from the bank. There are dozens of catapults available now, and we even have throwing sticks as well. However, as this is a basic tackle selection the Drennan Feederpult design should do for most situations. The Feederpult has a medium size pouch with holes in it for decreasing air resistance and a good strong elastic. With some practice, it is possible to bait up accurately at around sixty to eighty yards. Even particles can be put out to around thirty yards without too much spread in flight. Many catapults use ties to hold the elastic to the pouch and the catapult body but the Feederpult has prongs over which you push the elastic. This is an easier system and just as effective, and it proves a lot cheaper than buying ties each week. Elastics should last some while, but it is always useful to take spares just in case.

ROD HOLDALLS

In order to carry your rods and bank sticks and landing net poles to the lake, you will need to purchase some form of holdall. This will have to be big enough to take at least one pair of rods, an umbrella, a bank stick, a landing net and a pole. Probably, you will want some specialist rod bag to do the job. Today, most anglers leave their rod set up between sessions and for this you will need to purchase a holdall that allows you to carry made-up rods. Many of these will accommodate four rods as well as plenty of other things inside. As the best swims are often furthest away, make sure the holdall has a comfortable, padded shoulder strap. Length will have to be at least 6ft 2in to accommodate two-piece 12ft rods. Kevin Nash, Trevor Moss and Wychwood all make excellent items.

RUCKSACKS AND BACKPACKS

You will probably find that your collection of apparently essential fishing items increases with each trip and the normal rucksack will not be quite big enough. To cater for this Kevin Nash, Rod Hutchinson, Trevor Moss and Wychwood have each brought out large backpacks for the modern carp angler. The largest ones of these will carry all the fishing, cooking, camping and camera gear that you should need to last you for a long season. Just a tip here: if you are simply into short fishing sessions and do not really need such a large bag, go to an army surplus store, where you will be sure to find something quite suitable and far cheaper than in a normal camping shop.

TACKLE CONTAINERS

Successful carp fishing equals a multitude of small items which will allow you to exploit golden opportunities as they come along. If you do not keep these small items in reasonable order, they will be all over the place. An ice-cream container will help keep your optonics, monkey climbers and bobbins in one place. Stewart Plastics produce various sizes of tackle box for shot, line clips, sack clips and so on. Keep all your spare line and dacron spool in a separate box so that the line does not get caught in zips. Again, an ice-cream container will suffice. Keep the hooks in their plastic packets to avoid mixing up sizes and makes. A fly box with eight or ten divisions will hold your split rings, beads and swivels and as they have clear tops you can see at a glance where everything is.

SEATS AND BEDCHAIRS

Short sessions or stalking sessions require no seats at all or simply a piece of foam. Perhaps a garden chair would do – bought cheaply from Woolworths or Argos and perhaps recovered with something more sedate than the usual floral designs.

If, however, you are contemplating long sessions at the water, some sort of bedchair will be necessary to sleep upon. Various designs of sunlounger can be bought from Woolworths or Argos shops and are cheap and reasonably good value. You can buy replacement covers for most of these sunloungers to make these purchases look more in keeping with the bankside. However, for the really keen angler, there is little to beat the purpose-built bedchair that is now almost *de rigueur* on the top carp lakes. Fox are the established market leaders but there are several others available. The Fox Deluxe Bedchair is probably the best on the market but it is expensive and has to be viewed as a serious investment.

UMBRELLAS

Having spent all this time and money, there is nothing worse than suffering in bad weather. With the British weather as it is, an umbrella is really essential. Wavelock Umbrellas are probably the best, and the largest size you can afford makes sense. However, nylon umbrellas are cheaper and can be bought in smaller sizes. It is not wise, however, to economize too much on this vital piece of tackle. Steadefast and Hutchinson both produce excellent products.

BIVVIES – OR UMBRELLA TENTS?

Bivvies are not universally popular and are not considered by many to be an essential item.

Basically, there are two main designs available. The first is a wrap around/stormside design. This type of bivvy does not actually fit over the umbrella, but clips around the outside of it on to the ribs. Pegged down with or without the door shut, it does offer reasonable shelter against wind and rain. The second type of bivvy is the overwrap, which fits over the top of the umbrella forming a type of igloo tent. Securely pegged down, this will keep you warm and dry through gales or the coldest winter conditions. Canvas is warmer than nylon, but nylon is lighter and cheaper.

Do not immediately assume that you need a bivvy if you are only fishing in the summer or for short sessions. Bivvies do cost money and also take up valuable space in your backpack, so do not buy one just so that you look good at the water side. Nash makes excellent Stormsides and Canvas overwraps.

This extensive guide covers just about all the basics that you will need for carp fishing apart from your own clothing and items for

A typically recumbent carp angler.

weighing and photographing the fish, which are included in different chapters of this book. Obviously, the more advanced you get, the more money you will want to spend on ever more sophisticated tackle. You are the tackle dealer's dream and there is no shortage of excellent gear for you to spend your money on. It is always wise to read as many reviews as possible before buying very expensive tackle. See what the top men are using both in their articles and, if possible, on the bankside. Go to tackle shops and try everything out thoroughly – some tackle dealers will even lend you a rod for a day or two to see how you get on with it. Remember that there is a great deal of hype in the tackle trade as one company vies with another for the lion's share of the market. Do not be a victim of this increasingly commercial world.

CARP TACKLE TO WATCH OUT FOR

All rod-making companies have their line-up of carp rods and these are simply a selection of highly recommended ones. The Daiwa Amorphous is a tremendous rod even though it is expensive. One that does virtually the same job is the Rod Hutchinson Horizon rod, which is a little less expensive. The well known Armalite has a 3lb test curve and through action which many favour.

Carp reels of excellence are made by Shimano, Daiwa, Riobi and Dam. Old favourites were the Cardinal Series made by Abu, and if you can find any good second-hand 44x or 55s for example, they are well worth investigating.

The buzzer scene has had a tremendous boost recently with the updated optonics and brand new Foxes on the market. Also recommended are the Bi-Tech Viper and the new Delkim range. All these buzzers are very happily married to the Fox Swinger Range or to any of the high-class monkey systems on the market.

Landing nets are obviously very important and Gardener, Hutchinson and Chris Brown all make very acceptable models. Solar Bowloc is considered by many to be one of the best on the market.

Lines and hooks are generally considered two of the most important items in the carp angler's tackle box, and for many years Sylcast has been a general favourite. They are, however, now being pushed by Berkley in many situations. Nash certainly make some incredibly strong hooks, but the Drennan Super Specialist range are general all-round favourites. The Owner range is becoming increasingly important and Gold Label will also be a name to conjure with in the future. For incredibly strong hooks it is also well worth looking at the various designs in the Partridge range.

Comfort is also very important and the big Steads 50ft Wavelock umbrella has long been a favourite. It pays to choose a bivvy very carefully, and once again, Kevin Nash has produced one of the most heavily praised ranges. Kevin Nash and Rod Hutchinson lead the field with items that should suit every situation. At the moment, Cliff Fox's bedchairs and seats seem to be the market leader, though Lafuma make some very comfortable bedchairs.

It is obvious that carp anglers spend a very long time at the waterside and cooking equipment may be a consideration. The best bet here is to go into any camping shop or Army and Navy Stores and ask the advice of the outdoor experts. However, Coleman Stoves have become very popular with the carp angling fraternity and do provide a starting point.

8 Pike Tackle and Accessories

It is probably fair to say that no branch of specialist angling has altered quite so dramatically over the last twenty-five years as pike fishing. Of course, we tend to think of amazing advances in carp tackle, and this is true, but at least in the 1950s and 1960s carp anglers were thinking intelligently. This was not really the case with pike anglers – even though there were some very efficient men at the game. By and large, until the 1970s, pike tackle still tended to be as crude as it had been in the nineteenth century. Normal sea and boat rods tended to be typical pike tools, and any line would do providing it could haul up

Bob Church with a 30lb+ Fenland pike in the days when he was known as an angler rather than a tackle manufacturer.

an anchor! Hooks could be as large and rusted as you like and the Fishing Gazette bung was almost the size of a football. Even worse, the use of gaffs and gags was still quite common and it was not unusual to catch pike badly scarred around the chin and general head area. Indeed, the tackle and knowledge of today would have been almost incomprehensible a mere twenty-five years ago, and today pike fishing is truly a main line sport.

RODS

The pike rod now is a beautiful affair, and far removed from the stubby, solid glass objects of yesteryear. The general length of pike rods is around 12ft, though a few are still made at 11ft which are useful for boat work. However, for

A strong pike rod bends against a winter sky.

normal bank conditions, 12- or even 13ft rods give extra control and probably more casting ability. Generally, test curves start at around 2½lb and go up to 3lb, or in extreme cases 4lb. The longer and stronger the rod, the more likely it is to be able to cast big baits long distances. However, not everybody wants to hurl an 8oz deadbait one hundred yards off into a Scottish loch or a vast reservoir. If your type of fishing is a lighter, closer-in sort of work then buying the heavier rod will simply dull the pleasure of a hard-fighting, even if smaller, pike. Consider the type of waters that you fish before deciding on the length and test curve of your eventual purchase. Any rod will catch a pike, but the more delicate and precise the instrument, the greater thrill the battle will give you.

REELS

Much the same can be said of reels. If you are casting towards infinity, a big spool reel is a necessity. Reels are discussed on their own in Chapter 3, but it is worth repeating here that a sensitive clutch is an important point: a big pike can dive very quickly when it surfaces near the boat or the bank, and if the clutch isn't up to the job an insecure hook-hold can easily give way. Also, consider the strength of the spool if you are going to do much drifting or long-distance casting: plastic can shatter. Consider also the purchase of one of the more modern baitrunner reels: the baitrunner facility is absolutely excellent for giving a running pike line.

LINES

Lines are covered in Chapter 4 and I will simply repeat that it is vital to make sure that the line is in good condition before setting out to

Good, strong trebles securely attached
to wire and swivels.

has also been quite a bit of pioneering research on the use of double hooks and even large single hooks. I personally remember seeing one 32lb pike caught on a small roach simply nicked through the back on a size two single, and that fish certainly never looked like coming off once. Obviously, strength of hook is vitally important when it comes to a very large, hard-fighting fish like the pike, and you should never consider using a hook that you think will bend under pressure. Fortunately, now, most trebles on the pike market are extremely strong and have very sharp points.

Probably more important than the hooks themselves are the traces to which they are tied. There was a move some while ago to claim that heavy nylon was almost as good as wire. This is absolute nonsense and wire just cannot be improved upon. The important thing is to choose the right wire and make sure that your traces are utterly secure. Of course, it is possible to buy traces ready made up but these do work out very expensive. It is far better to find your own swivels, hooks and wire and do the job yourself. Do, however, take great care over this as a rush job can prove quite fatal, literally, to the pike. There is some very good wire on the market now, and the old days of undue tangling and crinkling are by and large over.

fish. This is especially important when pike fishing: if the line breaks because you have been careless and have not noticed some weakening or fault, then it is very likely that the lost pike will die. Whereas a carp or a tench might be able to shed a single hook, it is very unlikely that the pike will be able to get rid of two trebles deep in its mouth or even in its throat. For this reason, always buy line in bulk spools as this should be economical because you will not be afraid to change any of the line that looks at all suspect to you.

Hooks, also, have progressed a great deal over the last few decades, and a major bonus has been the introduction of either barbless hooks or at least semi-barbless trebles. There

BUZZERS AND BOBBINS

The emphasis in pike fishing today is on conservation, and no longer are pike allowed to gorge baits so that they are hooked deep in the gullet and unable, ever, to get off! A lot of the modern rigs feature sunken floats and no surface indication so it is vital to know immediately the pike picks up the bait. For this reason, buzzers in front of the reel are almost always used. The line is then fished tight from them to some type of drop-off indicator.

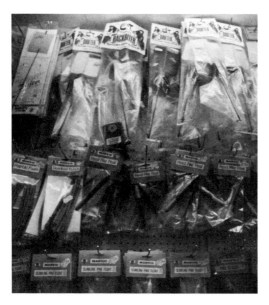

A massive range of pike floats.

These are marketed by several companies but certainly, for the good of the pike, I will recommend those made by E.T. These have proved to be totally reliable in thousands of piking situations in all conditions and on all waters. Never take any risks over bite indication, and do not wander yards away from your rods, chatting with other people, especially if the wind is high and you are unlikely to hear or see a take. A deep-hooked pike is often a dead one.

FLOATS

For reasons of pike safety, wherever possible I like to use a surface indication and the pike float is now far removed from the old cork bung of yesteryear. Moulded plastics have now produced semi-invincible floats of great delicacy and precision. By and large, the shorter, fatter floats are slightly more capable of supporting livebaits whereas the longer,

slimmer, pencil-type floats are ideal for use with deadbaits. For specialized long-range fishing, the Drifter float has now been part of the pike angler's armoury for a little over ten years, and can certainly get baits out to well over fifty yards. Instructions generally come on the packets of these floats.

BITS AND PIECES

There is probably no other branch of fishing (with the possible exception of the carp world) where the angler needs so many odds and ends in his tackle bag. Forceps, for example, are absolutely essential to take the trebles out of the pike's mouth, and many anglers carry two or three pairs, often clipped to the lapel of their jackets. Forceps come in a variety of shapes and sizes, and it is wise to carry a range with you to meet any unhooking situation that might arise.

The good pike angler will also require all sorts of small tools like wire cutters, or at least very strong, sharp scissors to be able to deal with wire traces. A hook-sharpening stone is vital for any treble points that can be easily blunted against the hard bone of a pike's mouth. A baiting needle will be essential to thread the line through a deadbait. A small screwdriver is also useful to deal with any emergency repairs that might be needed on a wind-blasted bankside. A sharp knife is always useful for dealing with deadbait trimming, and a tape measure is favoured by most pike anglers who like to know the length and girth as well as the weight of their fish.

An unhooking mat is particularly important for the pike angler because he must put the fish on something soft while he deals with what can often be a very difficult job. If the pike does move or squirm, it is vital that it does not injure itself on a hard, gravelly bank but simply moves over yielding rubber.

The bait also has to be considered, and whether you are transporting livebaits or simply keeping them alive, an air pump is vital. Deadbaits need equal care, and it makes sense to transport them in coolbags or freezer boxes, often with icepacks stowed around them. There is nothing worse than opening up some putrid deadbaits on a hot May day in Scotland when the chances of replacing them are virtually nil. It is also worth remembering that attractors and syringes are now commercially available to flavour your deadbaits and give you a little bit of an edge.

Finally, the tackle box should hold such items as a selection of beads to help protect knots at swivels and other sensitive areas. The normal pike bag will also hold a vast selection of bombs and leads to meet every situation. There will also be buoyancy inserts of polystyrene cut and shaped ready to make deadbaits float from the bottom. There will be stop-knot material – either a spool of power gum or some thin elastic bands. A torch is always a useful thing to have packed away, and if you are a boat angler, try to remember to carry a spare pair of rowlocks which can really help you out, even if just once in your angling life. If you are a keen lure angler, you will also need a lure box or two, depending on the size of your collection. Hook protectors are also vital to put over the trebles and stop them tangling. A piece of fine emery cloth is also useful for buffing up the blades of spinners, for example, to give them that extra bit of shine. Snap swivels are also important so that you can change yours over quickly and capitalize on any opportune situation.

Even this list of items is far from exhaustive and you will find that the experienced pike angler will build up the most amazing collection of odd bits of tackle over the years. Tape, string, toilet paper – you name it: every now and again the most weird and wonderful things will come in useful in the crazy world of pike fishing.

PIKE TACKLE TO LOOK OUT FOR

With so many pike rods now on the market, there is a great deal of choice for every budget. Towards the upper end of the range Tri-Cast Rods are winning a lot of acclaim. The Drennan Pike Float Rod is a very precise tool for fishing closer in, or especially for attacking rivers where sensitivity rather than simply range is the key. Armalite, North Western, Sportex, Daiwa ... the list is a very long one.

Trilene line is beginning to attract a lot of attention – especially the Big Game brand. Trilene XT will stand a great deal of hard work and has excellent abrasion resistance. Big Game is attracting a great deal of attention from carp as well as pike anglers.

There has been a certain amount of controversy in the press lately over the question of wire. PDQ has come in for a certain amount of criticism – probably unjustified. Certainly it has many big names to support it.

Drennan wire in all its breaking strains is a tried and tested favourite. Partridge very strong pike hooks are some of the best on the market, but they are closely followed by Drennan and Mustad. Marvic also produce several ranges of unique designs (mostly put together by that old maestro Vic Bellars) that are well worth a look for specialized situations.

Eddy Turner has moved heavily into the pike-tackle market, and certainly his backbiters and drop arms are now seen on most pike waters. Their sensitivity and reliability have won them glowing reviews.

9 Lure Fishing

There is little doubt about it: at this moment in time, lure fishing is the growth area in freshwater fishing in the United Kingdom. There are, I think, basically two reasons for this. Firstly, many fishermen understandably are turning away from livebaiting for pike, zander and perch. This is not a particularly pleasant side of the sport, and it is increasingly attracting the attention of the anti-angling brigade. All in all, livebaiting is on the fringe of acceptability in the modern period and our more sensitive anglers are accepting this. Secondly, it has to be admitted that there are many waters that tend to be livebait only and deadbaits work very poorly, if at all. Frequently, on these waters, lures are a proven taking method so they can be seen as a substitute for the less environmentally friendly livebaiting. Lure fishing is, therefore, partly a response to modern pressures and partly efficiency fishing.

I suppose that I should have added the third reason for the growing popularity of lure fishing: it happens to be great fun and tremendously satisfying. There is little to beat the sudden take from a good, spirited fish when slowly cranking back a lure. It seems almost impossible that any self-respecting fish will snap up a piece of wood, plastic or metal, but it happens with stunning regularity and each time the act appears like a minor miracle. Come to think of it, I should have added a fourth reason for the lure boom: in some

ways, lure fishing is a little like fly fishing. People simply find lures, like flies, irresistible. Their shape, their colours and their actions often catch as many anglers as they do fish, and there is tremendous excitement and satisfaction in building up a lure collection that will meet every fishing situation. Add to this

A lure is slowly worked back through a very likely pike slack on a big river.

Lure fishing can be much more exciting than the static livebaiting or deadbaiting approach.

the growing number of people making their own lures, and you will see that lure fishing even satisfies the basic instincts of the handyman. Possibly soon there will be lure-building guilds just like the fly-dressing clubs that festoon the country.

Until recently, English anglers lagged far behind the rest of the world when it came to lure fishing. By and large, the general run of English predator anglers did not understand lure fishing and tended only to use an artificial when all else failed. Of course, there have been notable exceptions and I am speaking in generalities. However, Irish and Scottish fishermen seem to have been far more convinced of the efficiency of lures for many decades. Perhaps their big, clear, rich waters are better adapted to lure fishing than our smaller, muddier ponds. There is certainly one consideration: you won't get far lure fishing if the visibility of your lake is measured in millimetres!

What has really opened up lure fishing for the English angler is the importation of American lures. For generations, the Americans have been way ahead of the game when it comes to lure fishing. Fly fishing and lure fishing are part of the American scene, and few Americans are happy using bait. As a result, countless thousands of ingenious American minds have designed plugs and spinners of every shape, pattern and colour and now that they are becoming increasingly available in this country the possibilities have widened considerably. The angling press has mirrored this development and several experts have been writing persuasively now for several years. Barry Rickards was one of our most important pioneers in this area, but he has been followed admirably by men such as Chris Liebbrandt, Charlie Bettell, Gord Burton and Mick Brown – amongst many others who would now not consider going out without lures on any type of water.

A selection of spinners and plugs.

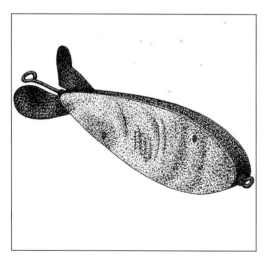

An Irish mother-of-pearl ferox lure. The brass gives it weight and the pearl ensures flash.

Today, the problem facing the newcomer is that there are so many lures it is very hard to know where to begin – though, of course, this is a much happier situation than in the old days when there was hardly anything to buy! Which lure works deep in mid-water or on the surface? Which lures have a violent action, and which a subdued one? Which colours are best for which fish? Is a plug better than a spinner? What size is best for what conditions and species? Should a lure be retrieved rapidly or slowly? Should the retrieve be smooth or erratic? All these and a host of other questions face the novice lure fisherman. Education is the only answer. The beginner can ask his tackle dealer – always presuming that person is a lure fisherman himself. More reliably, the beginner can read. There is little substitute for this unless he is lucky enough to come under the wing of an expert who will take him out on the banks. Most of the magazines now have an almost constant stream of articles on lure fishing, and some of them will supply back copies to complete a series. One invaluable book is the *Encyclopaedia of Lures* by Chris and Sue Harris (published by The Crowood Press, 1993). This gives a rundown of several hundred of the more popular lures now available and describes how they work and how to work them. Indeed, Chris and Sue Harris are now the primary importers of lures from America and Europe into the UK and you would be wise to get on their mailing list. Their catalogue is a real eye-opener and will provide Christmas present ideas for the rest of your life! I am not really going to say anything else about the choice of lures: this is not avoiding the issue – it really makes sense when so much information is readily available from two consummate experts in the field. Anything I say might simply cause confusion. It would be far better for you to phone Chris and Sue on 0692 581208 and listen to what they have to say.

My own experiences of lure fishing have mostly taken place when trolling on the big lochs of Scotland and Ireland. I have learnt that a lure that works one day might not work the next, and it is wise to take as wide a variety of patterns and colours and sizes as your budget will allow. For example, I remember one particularly sensational day when the only lure that worked was a black one. That night I spent hours converting my silver and gold lures to black by means of paint and black tape. The next day the black lures went totally fishless. In desperation I put on a green lure of the same size and make and immediately began to catch fish. That is one beauty of lure fishing: it is one of those methods where you have got to experiment constantly and ring the changes. You cannot afford to be mentally asleep when lure fishing or you will catch little. Keep thinking about the conditions and the water you are fishing over, and change

from one lure to the next if results are not forthcoming.

Of course, there is more to lure fishing than simply the lures themselves. You have got to remember that you need a certain amount of specialized tackle to go with the method, and here lure fishing expert Charlie Bettell fills you in on all the accessories that you will need.

LURE ACCESSORIES

'To start with I will talk line. Over the last few years I have tried many different brands of fishing line. Some have been cheap and fair, some were cheap and rubbish, some have been expensive and rubbish, some have been fairly priced and fairly good e.g. Sylcast.

Last year, for a change, I decided to try the American line, Berkley Trilene Big Game 15lb (0.15in average diameter). I was very

Lure fishing is not unlike fly fishing: you are always on the move, thinking and trying different things on the end of your line.

impressed with its lack of memory, and after a couple of months was very pleased with its performance. It kept limp and straight through "normal" plug and bait fishing. When using spinning spoons, though, it did coil up. When coiled, the line was a disaster, just like any other I had used previously. It, like its predecessors, had to be removed and replaced with fresh. When using spoons that spin, there isn't a line in the world that won't coil up if you do not use an anti-kink vane. When my newly modified anti-kink vane was used with my spinning spoons though, the birds stopped nesting in the line! It's a home-made 2in × 1in (50mm × 25mm) kink vane with a piece of balsa wood glued on each side of it. Because the add-on balsa is buoyant, the kink vane won't turn – not even once!

Towards the end of last season I was introduced to Silver Tread AN40 by David Smith. He told me the AN40 reacted in much the same way as the Berkley Big Game line, but it was thinner in diameter. The AN40 17lb line was only .0147in diameter, as opposed to Berkley 15lb line which was 0.15in in diameter. The AN40 20lb line has a line diameter of .0161in, which meant that I could up my line strength by five pounds for an added .0011in of diameter if I wanted. At the end of the last season it had passed all the tests with flying colours. I must point out that the AN40 is highly rated by most of the major lure companies in America.

For a lure company like Pradco, who own Rebel, Cotton Cordell, Bomber and Heddon, to promote AN40, the line must be good. A line that will stand up to hours of continual lure casting has to be an all-round winner in my view, as lure fishing has to be the toughest test for line.

When lure fishing, hooks must be set. AN40 does not stretch too much on the strike – some lines do.

This year I have used AN40 120yd puppy spools over a backing. I prefer to use a backing as it can work out very expensive using quality line to fill a deep spool, most of which gets wasted or never used! If I lose, say, 20–30 metres of line somehow e.g. snagging, I refill my spool. I always carry a spare puppy! I like to have a full spool for long-range casting, the AN40 being a supple, straight type of line, perfect for long-range work. Some lines that come off the reel spool in coils can greatly reduce the casting range, especially on a rod with small eyes.

Wire

In my view you cannot beat Drennan Seven Strand wire. I use 28lb test. You get plenty of wire for your money, so it can be changed regularly at very little cost. Using an 18in trace length, as I do, you get 50 traces from one spool. The only problem with Drennan wire is that when it kinks, it becomes very weak. It pays to keep a careful eye on it.

QED is a new wire to hit the headlines. It is claimed to be kink- and abrasion-resistant, yet I have had phone calls telling me how it kinks. In order to be fair, I phoned Sue Harris of the Harris Angling Company, which markets this wire, for her comments on QED. Sue informed me that QED is kink-resistant, not kink-proof! (Some watches are water-resistant, but try swimming while you are wearing one!) She sent me some QED to try out. On taking a length of QED off the spool, I found that it remembered where it had just come from i.e. the spool. Drennan wire has no memory of its spool. I found the best way to get the "coil-like lay" out of the QED was after I had twisted it into a trace, as it tended to coil up even more in the process of twisting it. I held one swivel in the left hand and using a twisting stick in my right, I twisted the complete length of wire via the right-hand swivel. After about ten turns, the trace length was completely straight, just how I like a trace to be (when twisting, make sure you twist in the right direction!). I found that QED whipped very easily (much more easily than Drennan wire does). Line of 20lb strength has yet to be put to the test by me, but I see no reason for doubting it . . .

The diameter of QED 20lb wire is .018in thick. The diameter of Drennan 20lb is .011in–.007in less than QED. Drennan 28lb is only .013in diameter which is still .005in less than the QED 20lb.

Swivels

I use Mustad, Berkley and Sampo ball-bearing swivels. I prefer these modern swivels to the traditional barrel swivels with just a single wire, twisted eye. Swivels have a lot of work to do when used for lure fishing. It's better to pay out extra and get the best. Note . . . on my kink vane, the Sampo ball-bearing swivel connects to the trace, eliminating any chance of trace twist.

Snap Links

I use American stainless steel Duolock snap links. Over the years I have not had any bother with them, which is more than I can say about some other links. The more pressure applied to the Rosco Duolock snap link, the harder it becomes for it to open! I use sizes ½in, ¾in and 1¹⁄₁₆in.

Reels

My favourite reels for lure fishing are my beloved Cardinals (3 and 4), now almost dis-continued! The reason I say almost discontin-ued is because the Derby Angling Centre bought up all remaining stocks. Anything that can go wrong with the Cardinal 3/4/4x can be replaced cheaply, including the bail-arm trip system. In seven years of use, I have only had to replace bail-arm springs.

When luring for big pike (heavier set-up) I use my C4. When luring for small pike (light set-up) I use the C3.

For trolling lures and bait I will use left-hand wind Ryobi T2s, Shimano 3500 baitrunners. Occasionally, I use right-hand wind multipliers for trolling, such as the Triton TLD5 lever drag, or my good old Shakespeare President. One other reel that is worth a mention for lure fishing is the Abu 1044. Although it is better known in the UK as a match reel, it does make a good lure reel, and even the Americans are pushing them this year.

All my reels have spare spools, although I tend to stick to one line for all my piking – 15–20lb. The reason for this high strength is that I mainly lure/bait fish from a boat. Some-times pike will go straight under the boats, causing line to be keelhauled, or a pike might go for a spin around the anchor rope. Strong line can help, not only in the prevention of such occurrences. Its strength also gives you added time to get out of the situation. When a pike does take your line around the anchor rope, open your bail arm and lift the anchor slowly, unwrap the line from the rope by passing it underneath the anchor. When free, close the bail arm of your reel and replay the fish. Take care while playing it, though, as your line might have suffered damage from the anchor rope. Before re-baiting, check 20–30ft of line for signs of abrasion.'

10 The Angler Afloat

I feel now is the right time to mention boat fishing, as a great deal of lure fishing is actually done out from the bank. Choosing a boat is a specialized task itself, and really outside the scope of this book, especially as most anglers simply hire out what is available on the water. If you have a choice facing you at the jetty first thing in the morning, take the one that seems to sit the most snugly in the water and not the one that looks top heavy, which will prove to be difficult to row and at the mercy of every gust of wind. Always check that there are rowlocks and a bailer and (if you are fishing relatively shallow water) adequate mudweights or anchors.

If you are thinking of buying a boat, take professional advice from as many boatyards as possible, and don't buy the first on offer in a newspaper column or at a sale. *Boat Fisherman* magazine (Burlington Press) is also a valuable aid to boat choice – even for the freshwater angler – and if you can get a copy of *Angling Afloat* by Stephen Harper (The Crowood Press, 1988) you are made.

I can, however, go into a little bit more depth with engines. Here, if you are thinking of doing any amount of boat fishing – especially trolling where distance is involved – then it pays to buy rather than hire. A good outboard can be hired daily at a reasonable rate, but by the end of a single season you really will have begun to save money by buying. Obviously, if you can afford it, it pays to

buy a new engine, with all the security and guarantees that this brings. But, again, like so many times throughout this book, you will probably have to compromise between what you want and what you can afford. If you have to buy an engine second-hand, for goodness' sake buy it from a reputable dealer, who will have taken it apart and corrected any faults. To be out in the middle of a large reservoir or loch in a mounting gale is not the time to find out that your engine is defective. Believe me, it has happened to me on more than one occasion. I speak from real experience here: twice I have tried to economize on engine purchase, and both times I regretted it dearly. The horror jokingly nicknamed the Black Pig was virtually my final undoing.

Whether buying new or second-hand, it is vital to make sure that the engine is big enough for the job you want it to do. All too often it is tempting to economize on the horsepower of an engine and find that it is not really up to pushing a big boat with two or three people in more than a flat calm. An overloaded engine soon begins to be fading one. Make sure that you keep up with the maintenance of your engine. Although servicing can be expensive, some people wait until their engine goes wrong. However, as I have said before, this can prove embarrassing at the least and fatal at the worst. Always take enough fuel with you when you go afloat. This is not so critical on a small lake but it

Some of the tackle needed by the boat angler – the dog is not compulsory.

does begin to matter if you are trolling on a really large water. It is surprising how quickly you can get through fuel, especially if the wind rises and you have to turn up the throttle. It is also wise to carry a spare funnel. These can blow overboard and without one it is easy to waste a lot of fuel, especially in a swell. Always make sure that your engine has a couple of spare shear pins strapped to it somewhere: it is very easy to knock the propeller hard enough to break the pin: without a spare you are absolutely doomed to a long row back home. No matter how confident you are in your engine, always take oars. There is no such thing as the 100 per cent fail-proof engine.

I, personally, always like to keep my engine to myself: I don't mind lending out any other bits of tackle, but an engine is a very personal thing. These 2-, 4- and 6-horsepower jobs are quite fiddly and precise, and it is easy to flood them or starve them if you do not know them intimately. You can lend an engine out to your best nautical friend and still find it comes back not quite as you last saw it.

Electric engines are absolutely superb for getting around small waters or even the large ones when it is very calm and you want to troll with a minimum of experience. In my experience, the Shakespeare range of engines is absolutely superb and the batteries are now pretty well adequate to last for a whole day's trolling, providing it is not into a stiff wind. There is no doubt that the turbulence made by an electric outboard is considerably less than that made either by oars or a petrol engine. In my view, the ideal combination, money permitting, is a petrol engine to take you to the part of the water you want to fish and then an electric outboard to troll you from then on. Expensive I know, but at least a target to aim for.

What follows is a list of bits and pieces that come into my mind in no particular order. All can prove vital on their day. If you are fishing a very large water then it really does make sense to take a full-sized Ordnance Survey map with you. This is simply to help you chart the quickest way from one point to another.

THE ANGLER AFLOAT

It is surprising how half a mile of journeying can be wasted if you don't map your route out beforehand. It is also a really wise precaution to take a compass with you in case a mist comes down and you find yourself marooned on one of the great inland seas of Scotland or Ireland. At least with a compass and a map you can get out of any situation.

You are almost certain to need boat rod-rests. It is possible to use rowlocks, but these are far from satisfactory. There have been boat rod-rests made in this country from time to time by various companies but now the best are imported, I believe by the Harris Angling Company. These, as far as I am concerned, are the best that I have seen, and although they are expensive they should last a lifetime, providing they do not go over the side. This last warning is a serious one. Over the years I have lost hundreds of pounds worth of tackle to Davy Jones' Locker, and nowadays I tend to tie anything at risk to the boat with a piece of twine. Thin, nylon rope is quite sufficient and it does mean that if a really sudden take occurs, strong enough to pull the rod-rest from the side of the boat, then all is not lost and you might even land the fish as well.

For the fish's sake a modern, carp-style unhooking mat is absolutely vital. For decades we have witnessed large, frightened, vigorous fish plunging around in the bottom of the boat doing themselves untold damage on the boarding or against the seat struts. Today, there is no excuse for this any longer, and if budgets do not rise as far as an unhooking mat then a couple of layers of thick carpet are nearly as good. A suitable net is very important as you can't really land any decent fish by hand – it is simply too dangerous to lean over the side of the boat in anything like a swell. It is certainly a help if the net is collapsible and easily able to be erected – even in a crisis. A short pole is also a good idea as a long one can create havoc in the heat of the moment.

Warm clothing afloat is absolutely essential: it might not seem too cold or windy on the shore but once you are a hundred yards out over the water you will find it is a different matter. There is no shelter out there, and the wind seems to cool as it crosses the water. Also, there is obviously no chance to walk about and warm yourself up. If you are buying your own boat it might pay to investigate purchasing a cuddy. These are rarely seen on English waters but in Scotland I have found them invaluable. A cuddy is simply a small, bolt-on shelter at the front end of the boat. This keeps all important tackle dry and is a superb windbreak. Also, if it starts to rain, the cuddy provides the most welcome of shelters. The problem with a cuddy is that it can catch the wind and have a detrimental effect on boat control.

It is a sensible idea to take binoculars with you in the boat. Part of this is simply to enjoy the day more. On remote waters it is possible to see a fascinating variety of wildlife and waterfowl through good standard field-glasses. Binoculars can do your fishing a fair bit of good as well, and often it is possible to pinpoint rising or feeding fish at several hundred yards' range that you would otherwise have missed.

Finally, and never to be forgotten, purchase a good-quality life-jacket. Most of these now are graded in terms of the weight they can support. Be generous with your weight allowance: remember that you will probably be wearing a lot of heavy clothing that will soak up water like blotting paper if you are unfortunate enough to go in. Make sure also that the life-jacket can be tied to you really securely because I have known at least one person and his jacket who were parted in the confusion of a shipwreck. Several firms now make fishing jackets with built-in buoyancy aids, and these are at least as efficient as the old-style orange and yellow affairs. The only problem with them is that they do not show up as well if search parties are looking for you.

11 Match Accessories

The world of match fishing is now a highly complex one, and the days are long gone when an ordinary pleasure angler could enter, pick out a peg and scoop a fortune. Techniques have advanced considerably, even from the 1970s, and tackle developments have gone hand in hand. One of those at the forefront of these advances is Kim Milsom, now regarded as one of the country's leading match anglers. In this piece, Kim runs through those essential pieces of tackle that top or aspiring matchmen need to consider. It is worth pointing out here that much of what Kim has to say is quite applicable to the pleasure angler or specialist man

Not all matchmen can fish as well camouflaged as this.

who is pursuing large roach, dace or crucian carp, and wants to use the finest and most delicate tackle.

MATCH RODS

'When a float rod is to be used with very light lines, several points should be looked at. Firstly, the tip must be soft enough to cushion the strike without any risk of "cracking off". In many cases this means using a spliced tip, but rods are now available which incorporate very thin, hollow glass top sections. These cushion the strike and avoid the possibility of a "hard spot" where the splice joins the main rod.

Secondly, if a big fish makes a sudden lunge whilst the tackle is already under pressure, there must be enough give in the middle section to absorb the shock. Beware of those rods that bottom out under surprisingly little pressure – a characteristic that should be avoided when better-than-average fish can be expected.

Thirdly, the rings must be inspected carefully. It is essential that they are of good quality. Cheap or poor quality guides will wreak havoc with light main lines. In a match, the line is constantly being used, passing backwards and forwards through the rings, and any weakness there will quickly make itself known – often with desperate results.

Fourthly, it is essential to check that the reel fittings are capable of holding the reel securely. This might sound obvious to you, but many types work loose with surprising ease. Again, just think of the battering the reel handle takes during the course of the match. Match fishing isn't like specimen hunting: the rod is constantly being used and a weakness here can destroy the whole match effort.

Finally, I would advise you to check that the handle of the rod is of a sensible length. When rods were made from heavy materials, handles were often made longer, presumably to help balance the rod. These days the rod should be extremely light (if it is not, look at another one) and the handle will simply get in the way if it extends much past the elbow when the rod is held.

A lot of these things can be checked out in the tackle shop but it is also a good idea to try to beg, borrow or steal some rods to test on the bank itself. Sit behind some of your friends or heroes and watch the way they use their rods and what make they have around them. Remember, a match rod is an expensive investment and it is fatal to pick the wrong one in an ill-guarded moment.

SMALL HOOKS

The general quality of small hooks has improved greatly in recent years, and now most makes are fairly reliable. This does not mean that they should not receive close attention before being put into use for they are the most vital of links between you and your fish. The points should always be tested. Running the point over a fingernail will "turn over" one which is too fine. Discard this at once, for these are the hooks which will burst a maggot, no matter how carefully you try to nick it on. Close inspection of hook points with a magnifying glass will also assist in spotting this problem.

Barbs on tiny hooks should be small and unobtrusive, so that the hook will slide easily into the fish with little pressure. Barbless hooks are often worth considering, particularly when speed fishing for small fish.

The "temper" of the hook should also be tested. Hold the hook on the point side of the bend (a small pair of pliers can be useful here), and apply pressure to the shank. Some hooks will open easily and others will snap. Most will retain their original shape and these are the

Things can become chaotic in the heat of the moment, so always make sure you and your equipment are well prepared.

ones that you want. Obviously, extra fine wire hooks cannot be expected to withstand the same treatment as forged hooks, and I should also point out that there is little need to test every single hook. One or two taken from any packet or batch should reveal any problems to you.

Many anglers use spade-end hooks, and the spades should be inspected extremely carefully. If they are too big, you may be adding a lot of bulk to a tiny hook and throwing everything out of balance. If the spades are too small, your whipping may slide off under pressure from a big fish. If you suspect that the spade is too small, tie one up, stick the hook

into something and pull it to destruction point. Then you will be able to find out whether the whipping slides off or stays put. This test is also a good way of seeing whether the line and hook are compatible. If the hook opens or snaps before the line breaks, it might be worth using light hook lengths with that pattern as the full strength of the line is being wasted.

The actual shape of a hook is largely down to personal preference. Any design which is useless is unlikely to stay on the market for long, such is the competition in the hook world. Crystal-bend hooks are probably the most popular shape in small sizes, but round-bend hooks also have a very large following.

HOOK LENGTHS

In recent years, the breaking strain/diameter ratio of lines has changed dramatically with the introduction of the copolymer types. Suddenly, a line with a diameter of .09mm (for example), which would usually break at around one pound, could now break at one and a half pounds or more, if made from copolymer. The advantages of this are obvious to any angler – not just the matchman.

One major point to bear in mind here is that many standard lines are labelled incorrectly! You will find that nearly all of them break at a higher strain than is stated on the spool. For example, many lines which are labelled around the one and a half pound mark will actually go at two pounds or even more. You must take this into account when swapping to copolymers, which have a far greater tendency to be labelled correctly. If you do not do this, your change to a copolymer line may end in tears as your new one and a half pound line will break at exactly that. Without realizing it, you are fishing much lighter than you have been used to doing.

The good matchman chooses the exact rodrest top to suit conditions.

The answer is to test the breaking strains of all your lines. If your old one and a half pound line does break at two pounds, replace it with a two-pound copolymer version. The new line will be much thinner and you will be fishing with the same strength.

One word of warning here: because of their reduced diameter copolymer lines are arguably less resistant to abuse than any other makes. When fishing in snaggy pegs some anglers prefer to revert back to standard lines whilst others will use stronger polymers. The choice is yours, but do be aware that the problem exists.

CONTINENTAL 'SEAT BOXES'

If you fish venues with rough, awkward banks, the adjustable legs of a Continental seat box come into their own – particularly when long pole fishing, where comfortable seating makes for a far easier day.

When choosing a seat box, watch for the "hand wheels" which make the legs higher. These need to be a shape which is easy to grip, for remember that you might be trying to adjust the legs when your hands are numb or covered in mud. A shape which is difficult to grip is therefore useless in all but tackle-shop situations!

An adjustable footplate is also a feature worth looking for. If the box is level but your feet are struggling to touch the floor, pole fishing, in particular, will be hindered. For this style of fishing especially, balance and comfort are absolutely essential to efficiency.

Most boxes will be constructed with ample space to store all of your tackle, but construction faults do occur, including leaving wooden drawers unsealed or unvarnished. This problem will only take minutes to rectify: remember, though, wood sealer is better than varnish as it will not add to the width of the drawer and make a tight, uncomfortable fit. If the wood is left untreated you are going to encounter problems when the drawers get wet, which is inevitable, and the wood begins to swell.

Another fault which occurs in some boxes is that the seat-covering material begins to split. The best way to avoid this problem is to keep your eyes open on the river bank itself and to see which makes suffer worst from this. Naturally, this is a good way to select all your match tackle: watch especially the better match anglers, for it is definite that they will have had a great deal of experience with different sorts of tackle. Many of them will be offered a great amount to test quite free of charge so that they have ample scope for choice. When it comes to

Using the feeder on a big winter river. This was cast out into mid-stream where the flow is quickest.

the match day, you can be sure that they will only rely on the best.

Finally, can I say that side trays are a distinct bonus when choosing your seat box.

TROLLIES

These need to be lightweight, robust, easy to assemble and preferably with pneumatic tyres. Tiny wheels should be avoided at all costs for very few river banks are as smooth and consistent as pavements. Some Continental seat boxes come with easily attachable wheels and a handle, which rules out the need for a separate trolley. This fact is worth considering if you think that you need both.

BAIT APRONS

A decently sized pouch for the bait is an obvious requirement, as is a flap at the top of the pouch that can be brought into use during rain. Easily accessible pockets for hooks, disgorgers, shot and any other little things that you might need should also be present on the apron around the maggot pouch. It is these small features that make for the ideal apron.

Also, watch out for the length of your apron, especially if you sometimes sit down when wearing one. Many are too long and the pouch is pushed up by the angler's legs which results in the great escape of the bait! Finally, if you require the apron to hold a catapult, make sure that there is somewhere to put one in the garment.

EYE-SHADES

In sunny conditions, a decent eye-shade can save a lot of eye strain and avoid a thumping headache by the end of the match. The main consideration is quite simple – is the peak large enough? This also applies to the baseball-style caps, which are probably more popular now than simple shades and have the bonus of keeping your head dry when it rains. Anglers who wear glasses will find a decent shade, or cap, particularly advantageous when fishing in the rain. (Author – What Kim says here is applicable to all fishermen: a lot of my fishing can be described as 'visible' fishing. That is, I like to fish for creatures that I can actually see. Polaroid glasses are obviously essential, but very often the sun is just at the wrong angle and a shade of some sort is essential for a full view of the swim. I have been laughed at by many of my big-fish hunting friends for looking like a matchman – but who cares when a 7lb tench is wallowing in the landing net?)

POLE ELASTICS

Virtually all types on the market are fine. Experience will tell you which size to use, but remember that elastic is perishable. Keep a close check on it and remember that the first signs of wear are usually located close to where it emerges from the pole itself. Wear and tear causes the elastic to go, but sunlight appears to do a lot of the damage.

DISGORGERS

These days disgorgers are fairly standardized, and, thankfully, the old metal ones have all but vanished. The more modern plastic ones which are now used are much less likely to cause damage to either the line or especially the fish. The barrel type is the best and it is well worth carrying the mini versions of these, if you are fishing for tiny fish.

HOOK TIERS

If you struggle to tie spade-end hooks by hand, a hook tier will be a very useful acquisition. Try to find one that does not leave the line kinked just above the hook – something that can be fatal when fishing very small, light baits. Hook tiers can seem awkward when first used, but practice makes perfect, so it is very useful to tie your first score or so hooks at home in comfort and warmth and in good light. (Again, a message for the big-fish man! It often seems that a big wary roach, for example, is more likely to take two maggots on a spade-end hook than it is on an eyed hook. This, presumably, is something to do with weight, but I also suspect the streamlining of the hook has some impact. Indeed, I would say that it is essential for the specialist roach angler to be able to tie a spade-end hook for those clear, cold conditions absolutely demand the finest possible approach.)

SILICONE SPRAY

If wind conditions allow, a much cleaner, more direct strike can be achieved with a floating line. Spraying the spool of line before use will help considerably with making it float for long periods of time.'

12 Swimfeeders

If any one river brought the swimfeeder to the forefront of angling equipment, it was the River Severn. This mighty water was stocked with barbel in 1956, when the Severn River Board of those days introduced several hundred fish from the River Kennet up to around 9lb in weight. For ten years, nothing really happened, and then the barbel population began to grow rapidly. By the early 1970s, hundred-pound bags of small barbel were commonplace, and matches were being won with the species up and down the whole length of the river. These small fish were voracious, and one method began to stand out head and shoulders above the others: the swimfeeder. Men like Fred Bailey began to

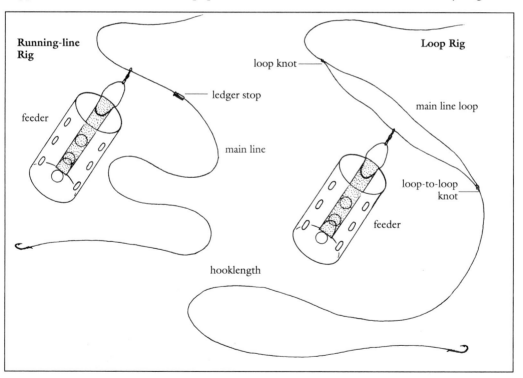

Feeder rigs.

pioneer enormous creations that could carry pints of bait out in minutes. The face of angling was changed for ever.

Today, any decent angling shop holds a bewildering stock of swimfeeders, and many different companies produce this most valuable tool.

The original swimfeeder was a block end – a swimfeeder that was closed off – that is the ends were blocked! These are perfect for carrying simple loose feed, especially maggots or a combination of maggots and, say, casters or hemp. There are several things to be kept in mind when buying a block-end swimfeeder for a specific task. Firstly, the feeder must be of the right size for the job in hand: if, for example, you are tackling a big river with shoals of hungry chub then a large, heavily weighted block-end feeder is what you need. If, on the other hand, you are looking at a slow-moving, gin-clear, very cold river and half a dozen large wary roach, then a small block-end feeder is what is required.

It is worth also bearing in mind the shape of the block-end feeder. In very quick water, you might find that a cone-shaped block-end feeder has more stability and is less likely to be pushed along by the current. It is advisable to carry quite a few different weights to go along with the block-end feeder, for it is imperative that the feeder is balanced precisely. What you are really aiming for is the feeder to be critically positioned on the bottom so that a taking fish lifts it with no trouble at all. It is worth spending a fair bit of time at the start of the session getting this right, for results will increase dramatically. When choosing the block end, also look carefully at the size of the holes. Most block ends are built with fairly small ones, which obviously slow down the rate of bait release. If, for one of several reasons, you want a quick bait release, then either look for a block end with large holes or simply enlarge them yourself on the bankside

with a sharp knife (do be careful not to overdo this, as you can cut the swimfeeder into virtual oblivion).

THE FEEDER-LINK

There are times when the traditional block-end feeder is simply too clumsy for very delicate fish, and for these situations the Drennan Company brought out their famous Feeder-links several years ago. The Feeder-link is really a mini version of the block end and built on a rather more sophisticated pattern. The Drennan design is very aerodynamic, casts well, creates little disturbance on entry, is pretty well invisible in the water and is perfect for introducing small quantities of bait to shy-biting fish. The Feeder-link comes in several different sizes and can always be made smaller simply by cutting through the body with a sharp knife, reducing the length as required. The Feeder-link is balanced by simply adding or subtracting shot on that little whisker of line that hangs through the tail of the feeder. The bigger versions have interchangeable weights that can be suited perfectly for differing current speeds. The Feeder-link is the perfect block-end feeder for stillwaters especially, and there have been times in the past when they have absolutely dominated the specialist angling scene for tench and bream, and even big stillwater roach.

THE OPEN-END FEEDER

The open-end feeder is simply a tube with holes in it with no blocks on the end. The idea is that it will carry groundbait to a precise spot over and over again, and deposit it close to the hookbait. The idea is to mix the groundbait quite dry so that once it settles in the water it expands and breaks free. The

A very big barbel caught in winter on the swimfeeder.

modern, aroma-filled groundbaits work perfectly with the open-end feeder, and items of bait can be mixed in as required. Hemp, casters and sweetcorn are perfect, but remember that maggots will wriggle to some extent, and tend to break up the mixture in mid-air if it is not packed tight.

There are many open-ended swimfeeders on the market and again the vital considerations are those of size and weight: how big and heavy do you want your feeder to be and how much bait do you want it to carry out? With shy fish, colour is also important. I have found, through observation, that certain large tench in shallow, clear water tend to keep clear of white open-ended feeders and prefer those that are coloured a weedy, dark green.

CAGE FEEDERS

The cage feeders are simple versions of the open-end feeders, and allow the bait an even faster exit. I, personally, am a great fan of the cage feeder, and tend to use it more often than other open-ended versions. You have to be careful, however, that the groundbait does not empty during the cast. Any jerking motion will result in disaster. A gentle, pendulum-type swing is what is required, and the groundbait needs to be packed in quite tightly. It is also said that the hook tends to snag a cage feeder rather more easily than a normal one, but I cannot say that I have found this at all. What I do like about cage feeders is that once empty, they offer little or no resistance to the strike or when being reeled in. The water simply passes through them, and they can be used rather like a straightforward lead. The other point strongly in their favour as far as I am concerned is that they also present little resistance to the current, and therefore keep their position well in strong water. For all these reasons, I have found the cage feeder to be the perfect tool for getting a lot of bait down quickly to the big groups of barbel or chub in fast, powerful water. I know what I say might sound a little unusual, but the cage has certainly worked for me.

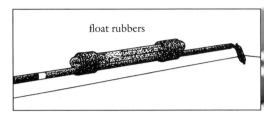

The simple way of attaching a Starlight.

THE MINI FEEDER

A new arrival on the market is the mini-feeder – either open- or block-ended – often only half an inch or so long. These are ideal weapons for carrying six or eight maggots out for very delicate, light-feeding situations. Their application is pretty strictly limited to close-in fishing, often for smaller species and generally during the colder times of the year, but the inclusion of half a dozen in a tackle bag could prove a lifesaver at some time or another.

BAIT-DROPPERS

The old method of getting bait down quickly to the bottom in a confined area was to use a bait-dropper. This is simply a canister that is attached to the hooklink and opens when it reaches the bottom. For many years, the swimfeeder seemed to drive the bait-dropper from the market, but more recently I have seen them begin to come back to the river bank. At least two companies market bait-droppers today and both are absolutely excellent. Obviously, if you are float fishing but you want to get bait right down to the

bottom in the swimfeeder fashion then the bait-dropper is for you.

Remember that a mass of feeders is now available on the market and beware of cheap plastic than can break up after just a few casts. Check the quality of the product and remember that the feeder really does take a battering through the course of a day's fishing, and nothing is more irritating than to see a feeder dissolve in flight. Check that the feeder is joined strongly by clips, staples or whatever. Check that the plastic is thick and not too brittle. Have a look at the links that attach the feeder to the line and make sure they are strong and thick enough to cope. Above all, it is wise to stick at first to recognized brand names, for then you know that the quality is pretty well assured.

There are still those who build their own feeder to give themselves an even greater variety of choice to suit every condition. That master of the feeder, Archie Braddock, has recently brought out his first book called *Fantastic Feeder Fishing*. In this, he describes how to construct your own feeders that will give you that little bit of an edge over many of the shop-bought ones available. Make no mistake, the swimfeeder in its many different varieties is here to stay, and the sensible coarse fisherman will learn which one is best suited to the many different conditions that we face throughout the course of a season.

13 Nets of All Sorts

Nets almost certainly preceded rods and lines as fish-catching equipment and, of course, they have now both developed commercially to comb the seas in swathes miles long. The damage that they do to all kinds of marine life is quite appalling. I have a very close friend who works in the North Sea for the oil companies, and frequently he comes across rogue nets that have broken away and are simply drifting, aimlessly, killing all manner of fish, bird and mammal life as they go. Dreadful, dreadful things, but then are not all nets – even our beloved keepnets?

Naturally, everybody applauds the advances that have been made in the construction of keepnet mesh and, certainly, the kind that we all used to have as children could be compared quite correctly to a cheese grater. At the end of a successful day (and I don't remember many) there would be a greater weight of detached scales than live fish in the bottom. And, of course, we all carried the net and its pathetic cargo to every new swim or hauled it out to display to every passer-by who expressed the least interest.

Again in the 1950s, apart from the horrendous knotted material used, there was no minimum size to the net. Economy, not conservation, dictated what was bought. Nets 18in long were common, and were only a step up from the Victorian fish kettles – which were, after all, only designed to keep fish alive and fresh until dispatched to the cookpot.

So nets have improved. From the 1970s technology was introduced at last and the pioneers were Fields from Cheshire. Their development of soft, knotless material must have saved millions of fish lives over the past couple of decades. Fish-friendly developments have continued as the mesh has

Look at the damage a net can do to fine roach.

become ever softer and the rings are no longer made out of damaging metal. Today, no angler should dream of buying anything but the very best keepnet on the market. But I still feel none but the match angler should buy one at all! Why? Firstly, the amassing of large numbers of fish in nets, however good, still causes a great deal of physical damage. Bream and rudd are particularly vulnerable to any kind of mesh, and tend to haemorrhage very quickly. Think also of those tattered dorsal fins that most Severn barbel display. Pike kept in a net will get their teeth caught and begin to twist so that soon their gills are lacerated. Secondly, at the end of the session, the net is very likely to be lifted out, and the weight on the fish at the bottom is sometimes enough to prove fatal in the long term – even if the fish is seen to swim off weakly when returned. Internal damage is not always so easy to spot.

Thirdly, seeing the abundant groups of a successful session in a keepnet is very likely to prompt the desire for a bag photograph. This takes time. It will probably involve removing the fish from the net and putting them on the ground, where they will come to even more harm. Fish already harmed suffer more wear and tear, and in hot weather the combined effects are frequently lethal. It would be naive to think that fish in a keepnet do not experience stress. The trauma of capture is increased several fold. How can we prove this mental damage? Well, it is as near to a fact as we can get that where keepnets are banned, the fish do feed in a less erratic, more confident fashion. Conversely, on a hard-fished match water, it is widely recognized that the poorest angling days are Monday to Thursday, presumably as the fish recover from the stresses of the two match days over the weekend. These circumstances are repeated over and over again, and certainly suggest to me that retention in a net puts the fish off the feed and certainly harms their mental make-up.

Finally, we have a very real problem with our public image. We are under pressure to stop livebaiting, for example. The use of keep nets is every bit as unfriendly a habit, and does give the anti-angling groups a very definite peg on which to hang their attacks. If we love the sport and if we love our fish we must learn to love them above our egos. Surely, this is a matter of education: for decades, keepnets were an accepted part of anglers' gear, but we do not burn witches any more, nor believe that leeches cure fevers. In just the same way progress can be made in the angling sub conscious. Books obviously date: it may well be that some collector reads this chapter in twenty or thirty years' time and marvels that I should spend so much time on a subject long since dead and forgotten. Let us hope so.

Presumably, there is little to be done about keepnets and match fishing. However, there is a vogue for more big fish such as carp and barbel to be caught in matches. Could these not be weighed on capture and be released at once? Bream are a particular problem: I feel a similar situation should apply here, but I do expect resistance on the grounds that released fish will scare the shoal. I cannot disprove that – there could be cases when such a thing happens – but my experience suggests this is not general.

There are times when a fish has to be retained for its own good. Barbel is the key example. All the barbel family from Asian mahseer in the East to Wye beauties in the West, fight out of their skins and need time to recuperate before being released back to cope with the current. In India, a stringer – a rope – is looped through the gills and the fish is tied to a tree until it recovers. Here, a keep net should not be used for fear of catching that dorsal fin: rather the fish should be supported by hand, upright in the shallows until it is felt to recover and work its body strongly. A pike tube could also serve the same purpose f the mesh is absolutely guaranteed not to catch those delicate fin rays.

LANDING NETS

Landing nets are quite a different proposition – although again I feel their use is general when it need not be. Let me explain: a landing net *can* harm a fish. If the fish is not quite played out then it will struggle in the net and lose scales or snag fins. If it twists, more and more protective slime is lost in the mesh.

Considering this, it seems that a lot of fish are netted when they could be landed by hand. I would go as far as saying that I land 90–95 per cent of my fish without a net. The process could not be easier: you play the fish out and then simply slide it into shallow water and up on to some feature like a soft mud bank or a nest of reeds. There is virtually always some nice landing pad to be found at the waterside. The fish is quiet, tired and still, and will be resting on something moist, soft

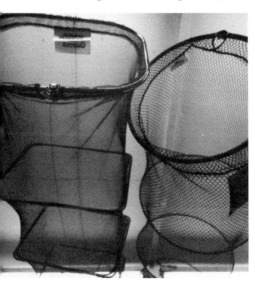

The two traditional shapes of net. The one on the left rolls less in a current.

and completely harmless to it. Then, all you do is simply bend down, locate the hook, twist it free with forceps and gently guide the fish back with your hand. The process takes seconds, and the fish is stressed as little as it is possible for it to be.

Strangely, I have never lost a fish during this process and I feel totally confident with it, and yet, come those blissful days when a whopper appears, I do like a net ready – just in case. But even when I use my net I take care. Do not net a fish before it is really ready, otherwise it will struggle and harm itself. Once a fish is netted, do not try to lift the landing net, but rather slide it through the water and place it in wet reeds or marginal weeds or simply in the shallows. Take the hook out, but have the camera all ready if you want a photograph. When the photograph is being taken, if possible hold the fish over the water. It is a simple job to lift it from the net, pose with it for a couple of seconds, have the shutter click a couple of times and back the fish goes, very little the worse for its experience.

There are now some super landing nets on the market, and most of these feature very similar points. The three obvious criteria to buying successfully are the considerations of size, lightness and strength. By and large, it is as well to go for the biggest, lightest and strongest net that you can afford. There will always be times when that little bit extra will prove useful. Points of weakness are often in the spreader block or at the point where the net is attached to its handle. Check these very closely indeed. An extending handle is often a great bonus, but do make sure that it will not jam or fracture. Try the net and its handle together and see if you can manage to wield it with one hand: this is very important for people who fish alone. Remember that there will be extra weight once the net gets wet and contains weed and fish.

This fish did not really need to be weighed.

even if I only want to keep a roach in it. Size and time are critical. Try to minimize the jail sentence as much as possible. Remember a fish has no eyelids and the sack can destroy or at least harm the delicate organs if it clings too close around the head for too long a period.

A major problem with all types of fish retention devices is that they allow the fish to rebuild its strength after the fight. This means that they can struggle very much harder when you try to hold them again: you either have to hold them uncomfortably – even danger ously – tightly or they will fall on the ground. The only solution is to let them straight back into the water without handling them at all.

I am pleased to see that there are continual developments in sack design and one good idea is to cut out the corners of the sack and substitute mesh. This allows the fish to breathe easily and permits very good water exchange. Draw strings are becoming increas ingly tangle free, and there are some enor mous sacks now available. Don't feel silly about buying the largest sack available: it could well save a fish's life.

KEEPSACKS

If you *have* to retain a fish, a keepsack is to most minds better than a keepnet. This is soft er and does not rub scales in the same harsh way. Nor does it catch in the fin ray to the same extent. However, the water does not always flow easily through a sack, and oxygen replacement can be a problem, especially in warm weather in still waters. Aim to peg the sack in deep, shaded water where the fish can lie as unstressed as possible. In a river, avoid both the total slacks and the rapids alike. Ensure the sack holds a stable position in a steady current and does not roll around.

Obviously, make sure that the sack is large enough. I tend to carry the biggest of sacks

WEIGHSLINGS

Do you *have* to weigh that fish? Is it a personal best or indeed anywhere near it? Is it a water record, or, indeed, anywhere near it? Are you entering this capture for a competition? Are you a part of any research programme into the fishery and the growth rates of particular fish? Have you caught the fish in the past and wish to check its weight gain or loss? If the answer is no to all these questions, may I ask, respect fully, whether you should consider getting the scales out at all?

Should the weighing be essential then a weighsling is important. It is often worth washing the weighsling after purchase in fab ric conditioner to improve softness. Many weighslings are now coated with an anti-slime material. Many have an air-flow fabric that allows quick water drainage so the fish is in the air for the shortest possible time. Look, obviously, for strong seams, strong cords and handles, for nothing could be worse than allowing the fish to drop from a height. Obviously, a sling needs to be thoroughly moistened before the fish is placed in it. Ensure that the fish is safely contained in the sling, for a full-blooded wriggle could send it tumbling to earth.

KEEPNETS

Size is all important, so buy the largest possible. Think carefully about the mesh design and choose as large and as soft a mesh as possible. This will help a good water flow through to the fish. Make sure that the rings are rigid, with no snags on them to catch scales or eyes. In my opinion, square rings are better than round ones as they will tend to hold the bottom better and not roll around in any subsurface currents. Always make sure that the net is pegged out well and does not collapse onto the fish. Some come with stretcher bars provided.

For the good of the fish, I am going to mention certain brand names that impress me. KeeNets seem to me to make some of the softest keepnets and landing nets available. I am a great admirer of the Kevin Nash keep-sacks. Ultracult make a quite fantastic unhooking mat. This comes complete with an inflator pump, and has inflatable sides to protect specimen fish whilst they are being unhooked. As the mat also floats, it can be used as a raft when releasing fish. There is also a very soft, internal protective cushion in the base. Indeed, using this, it is difficult to see how a fish could be better treated.

NETS TO LOOK OUT FOR

Steade-Fast, Keenets, Shakespeare, Daiwa and House & Co. all make very acceptable nets in mini, mono and micro meshes. Length is very important – do try to buy one 3m long. Remember that rectangular nets tend to remain more stable in flowing water. A large top ring is also important as this gives a spacious area in which to place your catch. The most conservationally sound net is the Super Mono-flow made by Keenet. The material is made from Super Mono-flow which is very soft. The bottom two sections are constructed from Safe-flow nylon: a dark material with holes for water drainage which is strong and safe, and has the added benefit of keeping the water for a long time after the net is pulled onto the bank. This reduces stress on the catch before weighing in. The net is a little more expensive than its rivals but should be considered.

14 Echo Sounders, Depth Recorders and Fish-Finders

Roger Miller checks the depth on the echo sounder. Note the rodrest and multiplier in the bottom right of the picture.

The fish-finder is one of the most controversial pieces of angling equipment in existence. Those who do not possess one completely misunderstand it, and feel that it enables the angler to cheat in some way. Their hypothesis is that all one needs to do is row around until a big fish is found, moor up, lower down a bait and catch a record fish. If only that were true! I can honestly say that of the hundreds of big fish I have had on my screen, I can barely remember more than half a dozen that have actually succumbed. A fish-finder simply does not work in that way, and any charge of cheating can be thrown totally out of the window as far as I am concerned – although I realize there is room for debate, and there will be people who disagree with me. All I can say to them is take a boat out on to a big loch in a strong wind, find the fish you are seeking on screen, moor your boat in a heavy swell over a hundred feet of water and just see if you can get it to take! It is even more difficult a task than I have just made it sound.

The echo sounder has come a long way since dear Bob Church lent me his in the early 1980s. At the time, Bob's was a good model that recorded the depth beneath the boat with figures flashed up on a dial. I forget the make, but I do know that on that particular Scottish holiday it served me reasonably well. At least, it gave me an indication of whether I was fishing over twenty, forty, sixty or even more feet of water. Though it was fairly crude,

it was a great help. It was that holiday that made me realize that I had to have a machine of my own, and in the intervening years I have actually owned four of varying types. My present recorder gives a screen image that paints in depth the bottom contours and the fish, which it shows in red, as opposed to black for all the rest of the information. The model that I rather fancy I will replace this with actually shows everything in three dimensions! What a concept – it will be like swimming with the fish in the safety and security of the boat scores of feet above.

My present machine is compact – the early ones weighed a ton – fully transportable and works off lantern batteries that last around a week. It has so far been totally reliable and proved rugged enough to withstand the nightmares of spring and autumn gales on the lochs and loughs. There is no doubt that this remarkable machine has helped me to catch fish (without actually putting them on the hook), but above all it has helped me to understand why I have or have not caught fish. Let me explain: without a recorder, I would know now as much about the lochs I fish as I knew ten years ago – that is, next to nothing. Thanks to my screen I now know the depths, the drop-offs, the gullies, the underwater snags, where the shoal fish tend to group and how deep the predators are lurking. The screen constantly flashes information and demands answers: why are the preyfish around the

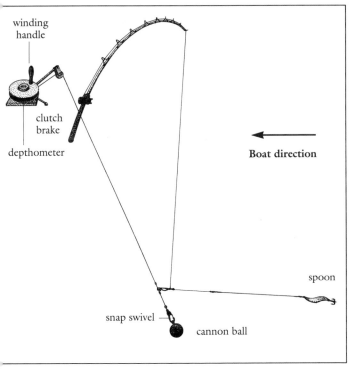

winding handle

clutch brake

depthometer

Boat direction

spoon

snap swivel

cannon ball

The downrigger system.

trout cages, why are the predators around the stream mouths or why does that particular bay always seem barren of fish? Trolling, a method that could be one of the most boring of angling exercises now becomes one of the most intellectually demanding. With a recorder, you now have to handle the boat (often in very adverse conditions), work the rods *and* make sense of what is being shown to you of the previously impenetrable depths. On very large waters I simply would never dream of being without one.

That does not mean that the recorder is only useful on waters fifteen miles long; it does have many other applications for all freshwater anglers. I was very interested, for instance, to read Paul Boote's new book *Somewhere Down The Crazy River*. The highlight of this work is pursuing Goliath catfish down Africa's River Congo. The interesting thing is that he located these specimens in the end by using a fish-finder. They were lying in a deep channel off an island, where there were many great trees lying as snags on the bottom. Paul eventually caught Goliath catfish after journeys that threatened his very life. The recorder played a great part in his success and without one all those months of suffering might have gone totally unrewarded. Cheating! I hardly think so: Paul had enough to do battling with the weather, the insects and diseases without worrying how to pinpoint big fish exactly along hundreds of miles of river.

The fish-finder can also be of great use in less exotic surroundings. A few years ago I set myself to catch some bream on the tidal stretches of a big East Anglia river. The problem was that there was absolutely no predicting where these small shoals of very big fish might show up, and it was only after I found myself a boat and began to patrol the river with a fish-finder that I had any success at all. It would still often take me two or three hours to find a shoal, and then the plan was to swing

Three beautiful trout that would probably have remained uncaught but for the Hummingbird.

back upstream of them and either trot bait down to them or feed fish into their midst. At last the fish started to hit the net. Cheating Well, I suppose I can see the truth of the charge here, but after all the whole purpose of fishing is actually to land fish, and after several weeks of constant blanks I was very grateful for the help my machine could give me.

A couple of years ago I lent my machine to the proprietor of a Welsh fishing hotel. He used it for a couple of days to chart the salmon pools and see what snags had been washed in to them by the winter storms. He found new trees deposited, and this knowledge undoubtedly helped his clients land salmon that they would probably have lost a the season progressed. Cheating? I hardly think so: what is worse than to leave a salmon tied by nylon in an underwater snag with a lure firmly embedded in its jaws?

Make no mistake, a fish recorder can help tremendously in assessing the potential of a water. A Scottish fish farmer friend of mine was called in to give a report on a remote hill loch that was reputed to have no trout at all. We took a canoe up to this remote water and set sail, the fish recorder between my knees. The water was in actual fact full of fish! They were simply lying quite deep in what was quite a cold lochan, and once sinking flies started to be used very nice little wild brownies began to be caught. Similarly, I was called in around a year ago to advise on the stocking of a fairly new gravel pit. The first thing I did was go out with my fish recorder, and the owner and myself were both amazed to find that the pit already had a massive head of good-sized fish. Full of confidence, I began to fish and caught good bream, roach and tench. The fish-finder had prevented the owner from wasting money and over-stocking the water.

There are several things that are essential in choosing a fish-finder. Top of my list must be mobility. A lot of American machines are designed to fit the owner's boat and are bolted into position – at least the transducer is. This might be fine if the owner of the machine is only using it on one boat and primarily one water. For most anglers in Britain, however, this is not the case. They will probably not own a boat, and will certainly not restrict themselves to fish in one water. Almost certainly they will want to hire different boats on different venues, and it is essential that their machine is totally transportable.

The next consideration is that the machine must be light. Remember, very often a long walk to a boat is required, frequently over rough terrain. If the recorder is not light with self-contained batteries then the journey becomes a nightmare. Ideally, the recorder will be small and light enough to fit in the tackle bag like any other piece of equipment. Mine, fully batteried up, weighs about seven pounds. Several of the older models used to work off a car battery and these were totally unwieldy.

Virtually all recorders now have the image thrown upon a screen. Beware of buying one of the older machines that had paper print-outs. These were unwieldy at the best of times, and in the rain you ended up being surrounded by yards of soggy-looking toilet paper! The screen is all important, and companies are making great attempts to secure ever brighter images. All images tend to vary according to light levels, but always try to choose the one that seems the strongest to you, even in showroom conditions.

Many machines offer features that really are little more than gimmicks. However, what can be vital is an audible alarm. This can be set to register sharp decreases in depth so that the machine lets out a warning once the bottom begins to loom up. This feature can save lives – especially on Irish waters where rocky outcrops can apparently appear out of nowhere.

It is also important that fish are shown in different colours from anything else on the bottom of the lake. There can be lots of confusing rubbish down there, and it is important that weed and fish are clearly differentiated. Also, do not try and save a bit of money by buying a machine that does not have a decent range. You might think you will never need to go deeper than a hundred feet, but it is surprising how restricting such a depth range can be. Ideally, choose a machine that allows you to see down to at least two hundred feet.

Of course, the home of the fish-finder is America, and it is a very good idea to try to obtain some American catalogues before finally making your decision. Several of the leading British specialist angling shops can

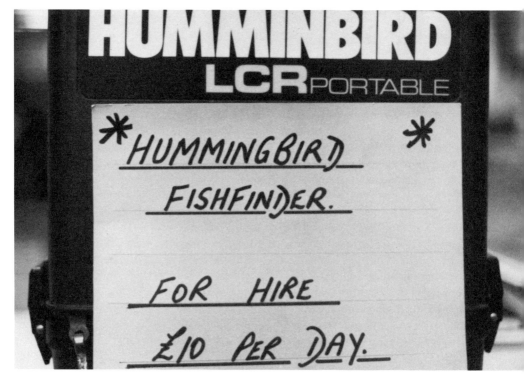

A common sign now in many tackle shops.

order the machines for you, and it is also wise to seek their advice. The absolutely infuriating thing is that the machines themselves are so much cheaper in America than they are over here. In fact, if you are thinking of buying one, it almost makes sense to fly out and make the purchase over there.

As a fish-finder is such an expensive piece of equipment, several tackle shops offer fish-finders on a hire basis, and it is worth while trying to come to some deal with them for an extended period if you are away on holiday. The trouble is, once you have used a fish-finder, you will probably not want to give the machine back, and you could have saved yourself quite a bit of money by buying one in the first place. One good idea is to club together with a number of friends and buy a group machine.

15 Anglers' Clothing

A lot of what I have to say now is simply common sense, and I do not wish to insult anybody by being condescending, basic or writing something that is obvious. However, I have fished in absolutely every kind of weather that the world can throw at us for over thirty-five years, and perhaps just one or two small points will be of use. Certainly, I well remember a particular winter in 1963 when I was still sent out fishing in shorts, wellingtons, one pair of socks and a couple of thin pullovers when the temperature was many degrees below! There were times when I sat and cried, and I would not want anybody to undergo anything like that.

It makes sense too in the summer, a period few anglers consider seriously when it comes to wearing sensible clothing. There are only one or two points to make, but they can often be overlooked. For instance, a pair of light thigh boots is absolutely ideal for an early-morning session when there has been heavy dew, and you are expecting to have to force your way through undergrowth to less accessible swims. Without thigh boots, your lower body becomes soaked through after a mere twenty yards or so, and the rest of the morning can be a very chilly, unpleasant experience indeed – at least until the sun comes up and dries you, which might be some hours in the future. Those really light thigh boots are no trouble to wear, and as the day gets hotter the top lengths can easi-ly be folded down so they don't cause you sweating and discomfort.

Moisture can be a problem in the summer even if the early skies are blue, and for that reason I always tend to carry either one of two light jackets. One is a Peter Storm rainproof which weighs just a few ounces and yet will keep out a real thunderstorm. It has a hood and it lets you 'sweat' without any problems of condensation. If for some reason the Peter Storm is not to hand, then I will take the lightest Barbour coat, and this again weighs only ounces and will keep out at least three or four

Thigh boots can be very useful, even in summer.

hours' light to medium rain. Even if the heavens do not open, both these jackets are excellent as groundsheets to sit upon for those times when you really want to travel light.

A light hat does keep off the sun and, by giving a little shade over the eyes, probably helps fish spotting too: and that is important even if personal health is not! Equally obvious will be this warning about biting insects: anybody who has fished in Scotland will know that they can quite easily drive you off the water from dusk right through to mid morning. There is absolutely nothing worse than midges or horseflies, or a combination of the two ... and mosquitoes aren't very nice either! There are many brands of anti-insect lotion on the market, but many years' experience has led me to believe that Jungle Formula is just about the best that money can buy. It is pretty evil stuff to get on your hands and clothes, and it feels as though it will do permanent damage – but it doesn't – or at least only to the insects. I find that one application will do for several hours and is very effective. I have got to say that all manner of remedies have been passed on to me over the years: some have sounded absolutely repulsive, but even so they have not really worked nearly as well as Jungle Formula.

Finally, should you be new to night fishing, remember that even the warmest periods of weather will throw up a cold snap late in the night and around dawn. It is unbelievable how far temperatures can plummet, and if you are inexperienced enough to set out with only light summer clothing you will live to regret it for a few hours.

Late autumn and winter clothing is, of course, much more specialized and no matter how inclement a summer's day can suddenly become, it is unlikely to kill you. The same cannot be said for winter. There have been three developments in outdoor clothing that have, for me, changed winter fishing from

being an ordeal into something to be actively enjoyed. All three are so important I hardly know where to begin. . .

Feet! Cold feet have driven this particular angler off the river bank more times than he can remember over the years. Gone are those days of thin wellingtons and fisherman's socks that manage to keep the cold at bay for around thirty minutes. The modern moon-type boots are the thing! Cold feet are a thing of the past. Again, warm feet are so important that I must mention the brand name that I use. Skee-Tex Boots have been on my feet every winter fishing session now since 1985! And they are the same pair! I have had to change the inner fleecy lining every couple of years, but the cost of that is pretty small considering the benefits that they bring. They are not that easy to walk in and their grip is not perfect on slippery banks, but if you are reasonably fit and tread carefully I know of nothing better.

Now, on to the outer shell. Again a brand name – the Bob Church one-piece waxed suits have been my companions for virtually ten years. I find one suit does me around two or three seasons, but that means very intensive fishing and not looking after it at all. There are other makes on the market, and I am sure they are the equal of the Church pattern. I only mention Bob's because his suits have really done the business for me over the years. Even so, they are not perfect. If I had control of his design, I would probably put a double thickness bottom patch in and treble thickness around the knees. It is these areas that seem to take a lot of the wear and tear and go first. I would also put a couple of hand-warming pockets up near the top – much in the way of a Barbour jacket. There are numerous times when you do not want to wear gloves but would really like somewhere snug to stick your hands for a minute or two. Whatever make you opt for – and go without at your

The Bob Church jacket is the author's choice.

defy even the British weather to penetrate thermals, trousers, a pullover or two, a one-piece wax suit and moon boots.

Gloves, however, are, a tricky issue and I personally have never found a pair that really suits me. It is common to see anglers use mittens with sawn-off finger pieces: as far as I am concerned they accentuate the horror of cold in the exposed extremities. Most gloves just seem to get wet, and once that happens they are worse than useless, but it could be that somebody out there has a secret. I seem to find that at the start of the session my fingers get very cold and painful for half an hour or so and then warm up and remain warm for the rest of the day without any need for gloves whatsoever.

peril – check that the lining is of good quality and is there in ample quantities. Also look to see if the seams are generous: it is in this area that most jackets seem to go first. Some sort of elasticated cuff is vital to stop water running down your arms, and a really good hood is also essential. Big, waterproof pockets are vital. Check that there is plenty of room in the leg for boots to fit underneath. On the question of size, always err towards the large, for there will be some days when you want to get a good few pullovers underneath as well.

The third piece of good news is the advance of various types of thermal underwear. I tend to go for the one-piece, babygrow-type of outfit and wear a vest and underpants underneath, but the choice is very much up to you now there are so many varieties on the market. I

I ought to mention that the fishing tackle shop is not necessarily the best place to buy winter clothing for anglers: not every shop can afford to stock every company's entire range, and it is sometimes wise to have a look at the catalogues before making your decision. Never neglect your general outdoor camping, skiing-type shop: these people cater for mountaineers and trekkers, and are likely to know the sort of clothing needed for very low temperatures. Their stock is often extensive even though their prices are frequently on the high side. Bearing this in mind, it often pays to shop at the start of the summer with winter fishing in mind.

In Chapter 9 (*see* page 81) Charlie Bettell wrote about lure fishing accessories: it is perhaps wise to mention here some essential trolling precautions. Never, repeat never, go afloat on any water, large or small, without a life-jacket of some sort. No matter how still, warm and friendly the water may look, conditions can change rapidly, and disaster can strike. Your first mistake could easily be your last. There are several suits these days with built-in safety jackets, and these are well worth considering if you do a lot of fishing afloat. Failing that, buy a simple life-jacket and wear it all the time. Also, remember to buy a large size, for it will have to go over pullovers and one-piece jackets. Zip it

Protective clothing that has seen better days!

up, tie it tight and wear it at all times: never use it as a cushion for a hard boat seat!

These are the sorts of clothes that I wear and I hope you do not mind me taking up space by saying so. Of course, on today's match scene these drab, green, brown, generally murky, unattractive things are not the sort of thing wanted but I have no experience of the highly coloured, bri-nylon affairs labelled 'Team Flash' or whatever. Perhaps they are nice and warm and waterproof, but what I do know is that they make an angler stand out like a sore thumb on the river bank, and this cannot be a good thing. Fish in the water can see an angler conspicuous on the bank. Perhaps not every fish in every situation will see

you and flee, but if only 10 per cent do so each season then they are fish lost that you could have caught. Why on earth take the risk for the sake of vanity?

CLOTHING TO LOOK OUT FOR

Wychwood, Hutchinson and Church, amongst others, all make excellent protective clothing. The thermal boot scene is very complicated and Skee-Tex have certainly stood the test of time. Thermal 88 make very warm boots and Boon 80 are probably the favourite big specialist angler's boots.

16 Anglers' Luggage

Every angler needs something to carry his tackle in and upon which to sit at the bankside. For generations, this was the job of the wicker box or creel. For some reason, these have gone out of fashion, and the only places you will now find them are antique shops or at car boot sales. They can be bought for a very reasonable price, and I have seen some on sale in excellent condition. Quite why the wicker basket went out of the freshwater fisherman's life is hard to understand. They were capacious and quite light for their size. They were hard wearing and comfortable to sit on and, best of all, the open weave of the material allowed smells to disappear. You could also wash them right out and they would dry in the sun in an hour or less. The wicker basket suited everyone – matchman, specialist or pleasure angler, but now things have changed dramatically and an angler's fishing persuasion can quite easily be seen by the luggage that he carries. A matchman has to have one of the large, Continental, moulded plastic boxes. Equally, the more specialist angler must be seen with a large rucksack and a designer-built chair or bedchair. The pleasure angler tends to fall uncomfortably between the two stools – as it were.

Having a rucksack is a good idea, and in a naive way I even helped to pioneer it myself back in the late 1960s when I began to carry limited gear for roaming roach and chub fishing in the old bag that I used for my paper-round back in the early 1960s. I found that this was far easier to carry than any wicker box and all the gear plus a loaf and a small stool could easily be accommodated. Now, of course, rucksacks are commercially made for the angler, and they are excellent items.

One of the more important things to decide when buying a rucksack is the size that you will need. It is pointless buying one too small for then you will have endless problems cramming everything in. Equally, buy one too big and you run the risk of taking too much and adding on to the weight. Think carefully and reach a happy compromise which should do you for 99 per cent of your fishing.

Most of the purpose-built rucksacks are of very good quality, but do check the material and the stitching for robustness. Rucksacks go through a great deal of wear and tear throughout the course of a season, and there is nothing more annoying than finding rips or having the seams disintegrate. Also check the shoulder straps and make sure there is ample padding with foam rubber or something similar. If you are walking long distances with the rucksack, you do not want the straps to bite into your shoulders – especially through light summer clothing. Ensure that the rucksack is easily carried – not just in the shop when wearing a pullover, but also during the winter if you have got a thick one-piece suit on. For this, the straps should be widely adjustable.

The modern angler carries a lot of gear and needs strong luggage.

Check that the rucksack has all the different pockets that you require. It is very nice if you know that your scales, floats, swimfeeders and everything else are all separate and easily accessible. There is nothing worse than the mass of tangled gear all wrapped together by discarded nylon lurking at the bottom of a basket. If you carry a camera – and virtually all of us do these days – it is wise to see whether there is a totally waterproof and even padded compartment for it. This certainly gives you peace of mind when walking over tricky terrain or when it is raining hard. Of course, the material should be pretty well waterproof itself, and you should make sure that it is easily washable because the amount of grime and mud that clings to the rucksack is amazing – especially when it rains and the bank is

muddy. It is a great help if the rucksack has good strong straps that allow you to tie your chair to it. This is a trend these days: carry the gear in a sack and sit on one of the camouflaged, purpose-built fisherman's chairs.

When choosing a chair, make sure that it is what you want: if you fish a lot of long sessions, it makes sense to buy something sturdy and comfortable. If, on the other hand, you are a roving, short-session type of angler then a big chair only adds unnecessary weight to your kit. Think carefully about this and reach a sensible compromise. Today's chairs are generally comfortable, rugged and easily adapted to different bankside conditions. Here, I must voice one little regret of my own. For many years – twenty-one in fact – I have used one of the old Paka-Seats that were made, I think, by Efgee Co. The concept behind these was that the tackle could be put in a compartment that was built into a small, low, comfortable chair. There are, however, some problems with the Paka-Seat. Space is limited and the chair is quite low and not absolutely comfortable for a big man for many hours. However, it is an incredibly light-weight piece of kit and certainly takes most of what I need for most of my trips. Also, considering the number of times that I have fallen asleep on it, the comfort can't be too bad either! Sadly, it seems that the Paka-Seat is no longer available. People just stopped buying it. The trend had moved on to seemingly more sophisticated gear. I still think this is a shame and I look forward to some enterprising company bringing out a new, improved seat-cum-basket all in one. It will certainly make my life easier and stop me having to repair my aged Paka-Seat every year or two.

LUGGAGE TO LOOK OUT FOR

The luggage market is a congested one at the moment but Rod Hutchinson Tackle Developments make excellent holdalls and rucksacks. The Kevin Nash range is also well worth investigating and the new Titan rucksacks are attracting a lot of attention. Probably the market leader on the specialist side is still Wychwood, who make a very wide range of luggage for the specialist angler.

The situation is even more confusing when it comes to the Continental seat boxes. Shakespeare, Boss, Tubertini, Daiwa, Browning, Eurobox, Water Craft and Steadefast are just some of the firms making boxes for today's match angler. Price is very much the key here. To a large extent the more you pay, the more you get and it is worth while going to as large a tackle shop as possible and reviewing as many as possible for yourself. As far as trolleys are concerned, Combo and Prestige are getting quite good write-ups, but it is worth looking at the Tackle Box Harness which is marketed by Harple Design Limited. The seat box is fitted on to a cloth base and held in place by two straps. There are two more padded straps that allow the angler to carry the box almost like a rucksack. The harness is quick and easy to use and is comparatively cheap.

Continental Boxes

Firstly, it is a common mistake to feel obliged to buy the biggest Continental-style tackle box on sale in the tackle shop. Remember that even one tray of the lid section can hold a lot of pole winders and general tackle. There are several important points to consider when you go and buy your box. It is very important that all the clasps and fastenings are strong and work reliably. If drawers open accidentally then spillages are almost inevitable. Do make sure that all drawers and lids are securely closed before carrying the box to or from the water. Spilling tackle is a nightmare. Make sure the box can be lifted without the heavy lid sections making it feel unbalanced.

Some of the Continental boxes can appear to be on the high side for shorter anglers, especially when they are seated and fishing with a pole. An answer can be to remove one or more of the lid sections and put them by you on the bankside. Check if this is possible.

When fishing, if the box you have bought has adjustable legs, make sure that everything is level. Do remember that if you are fishing on a soft bank, the legs will sink down considerably, so get everything into place and make all the adjustments that you need before starting to fish.

Some boxes come with footplates that can be very useful as they rule out the need for a full platform. However, some of the top anglers carry a platform with them as footplates can be hard to put into place. The platform can also double up as a place to stand bait.

The market is now very busy with new designs of Continental boxes and the different features that they offer are mind-blowing. It pays to take your time and consider all the options very carefully. Make sure that you want the latest gimmicks being offered – otherwise you are simply paying out money unnecessarily. These new-style boxes are very strong and rugged and should be virtually rust- and rot-proof. It still makes sense, however, to take good care of them and wipe them down frequently to stop mud creeping into the hinges.

One drawback is that these boxes tend to weigh a fair amount, and this can necessitate the purchase of a fishing trolley. These are now made by several companies. Do ensure that the base will take your box comfortably. Good, broad wheels are also important if you are likely to be taking a trolley over uneven or boggy ground. Make sure that the trolley is made of tubular steel so that it is as light as possible and it is a great help if the wheels come off quickly and the whole construction can be folded flat for easy transportation. Some trolleys come fully rust-proofed, which is an important consideration in a damp British winter. One of the most important things to check is all the joins and areas of conceivable weakness. In my opinion, it pays to stay away from anything that is welded as this is a potential trouble-spot in the future. The fishing trolley undergoes a great deal of hard use throughout the course of its life, and any weaknesses will show up very soon after purchase.

Trolleys that convert into platforms for boxes are becoming more popular and these should also be considered. They are versatile and reasonably well priced, and some of the best ones only take three to five minutes to convert from a trolley into a platform. The only problem is that they tend to be on the heavy side.

17 For The Record

SCALES

I suppose most of us began weighing our fish in the early days on the Little Sampsons. For many years, mine, which weighed up to 4lb, did me well, and it was only with my first carp that I had to invest in a set that went to 7lb! I soon wished I had bought the 14lb set and before long I ended up with all three! There is nothing really very wrong with the spring balance, and it is interesting that most serious anglers prefer the dial scales. In fact, my largest ever pike was weighed on a spring balance, and when this was later checked it was found to be accurate to within an ounce – not bad for a fish well into the thirties! One pleasing thing about the spring balances is that they are light and compact, and therefore take up little room in the tackle bag. Provided they are well oiled and water and rust are not allowed in, they can give years of excellent service, so my advice is not to neglect them.

However, dial scales certainly have the greater following and I suppose the Avon range is the firm favourite of most people. Interestingly, the most popular Avon has been uprated from 32lb to 40lb recently to cope, I suppose, with the recent upsurge in big carp and pike catches. This welcome eight pounds must make it more popular still with a great many big-fish anglers. However, there are two problems with Avons that I have never really been able to reconcile. Firstly, the

colour-coding system on which they operate does cause confusion, especially when it is read by inexperienced anglers. Quite frequently, fish have been recorded a whole circulation above or below their true weight, which can make a great deal of difference. It is not unusual to see a fish in the angling press which is obviously eight pounds light of the

Avons take the weight.

weight claimed – often with no malicious intent on the part of the captor.

Secondly, I have found in the past that the all-important weighing hook is far too weak. I am sure I am not the only person to have had problems with the hook bending under the weight of a hefty fish. This is where I must praise the dial scales marketed by Kevin Nash. These are very large and very easy to read. The scales which I have used have weighed up to 56lb and to 112lb, and they have been remarkably accurate. Equally important, the weigh hook on the Nash scales could take a shark! It simply could not bend under the weight of virtually any freshwater fish in the world – a major advantage.

If the Nash scales have one weakness it is that they weigh in 4oz divisions at the 56lb weight. This should be enough for most people, but there is the outside possibility that you might one day be called upon to weigh a record fish. For this reason it is possibly worth looking at the Reuben Heath scales. These weigh a mighty 60lb in 1oz divisions, which makes them ideal for any potential record carp or pike.

Thick plastic makes a good weighsling.

Richard Walker's 31lb common carp is measured. Note the Mitchell 300 reel and the hand-built split cane rod beneath the giant fish.

When choosing your scales, bear in mind the importance of clarity, robustness and resilience to water and general damp. Also do check that hook. While you are in the tackle shop it is a good idea to buy a scales pouch which will keep this delicate piece of engineering free from vibration and the wet.

If you have caught and weighed a very, very special fish and ounces are of desperate importance to you, it is worth noting that the Weights and Measures Department will check your scales for you. This happened recently to a friend of mine when the brown trout record stood at 19lb 9oz. On a far northern loch, John caught a trout that weighed 19lb 4oz in the boat. His scales were checked and the actual weight of the fish turned out to be a meagre 2oz below the record. A very close-run thing!

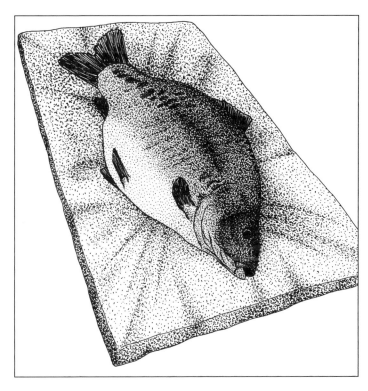

Never lift a big fish too far from the ground: its internal organs are unprotected in a fall.

into the ground right by the fish's nose and another into the ground right by the fork of the tail. Then measure the distance between the two sticks and you have the genuine distance.

TAPE MEASURES

There is very little to be said here. Virtually any soft tape measure will be quite adequate for all occasions, and it is worth while measuring certain fish to gauge an idea of their weight-to-length ratio and their general condition. What is important is to know how to measure a fish correctly. If you simply lay the tape measure from fork of tail to snout then it follows the outline of the fish and up to an inch is added to the length. To avoid this false reading, put one stick

CAMERAS

Most people today have one of the light, easy-to-use, new-style compact cameras. Most of these are auto-focus and auto flash, and many incorporate a zoom lens. *Which?* magazine reports quite frequently upon them, and you can find a very good, very reliable model at a reasonable price. These are being constantly updated to win a share of what is a very competitive market, and it would be unwise to single out any particular make as the leading

117

A big barbel is unhooked ready for weighing and photographing.

brands change so frequently. For many anglers, however, working under difficult conditions, a compact is simply not enough.

A really serious angling photographer will want an SLR camera. This is a single lens reflex set-up that actually shoots what you see through the frame. These cameras are more professional, they give better quality photographs and are more adaptable. With an SLR camera you can use a greater variety of lenses and filters and explore far more overall potential. An SLR will be heavier than a compact camera, but not prohibitively so. Also, a SLR system will be more expensive, but you should be able to afford to buy a body and two lenses if you shop around wisely. The modern generation of SLR cameras tends to be auto-focus. Originally I was

against this concept but then I had a summer's experience of using a Minolta, and this changed my conservative opinions. I found the auto-focus option very quick to use and excellent in those half-light conditions when manual focusing could be a very fiddly job. Also, the auto-focus makes the camera ideal for strangers to use: you hardly need to know anything about a camera to take a decent shot. Most auto-focus cameras also offer a manual option as well so that you can take all manner of high-tech shots that are beyond the auto-focus range. Certainly, Canon and Minolta are two makes that I would happily recommend.

For the bulk of my photography I still use my Olympus manual focusing system. The OM2s and OM4s are very tough, very reliable and somehow I feel are better for those pin-sharp shots that we all love to see. However, I am overly conservative and also arrogant in thinking that my eyes are sharper than the computer of an auto-focus camera. Good Olympus bodies can be found second-hand now, often with a guarantee. These are a very good, sensible buy.

Lenses

For a number of years now, we have had zoom lenses which are very good, very useful and very compact. I use several myself, though I doubt if they are quite as sharp as a fixed-range lens. When I want everything perfect I will go for a standard 50mm lens or whatever the situation demands. Either fixed or zoom, the serious angler photographer will want a whole range of lenses at his disposal. A 24mm or a 28mm lens is essential for wide-angle shots of lakes, rivers or action inside boats. A 50mm lens is the perfect one for most portrait shots. A 200-, 300- or even 400mm telephoto lens is what you need for long distance shots of fish basking or of wildlife. A macro-lens is also very nice to have so that you can zoom in close and take pictures of fish scale damage, for example, or the colours of a zander's eye! Ideally, it is wise to buy the same make of lens as the camera body, but this can prove quite expensive. The independent lens-making companies offer some terrific products and I have been very happy with lenses made by Sigma, Vivitar and Tamron. There are many others to choose from, often at a far cheaper price.

Filters

It is always useful to put a plain skylight filter on any lens you buy as this will protect it from scratching and have little or no effect on the photographs you take. I also find a polarizing filter very useful indeed. With this it is possible to take shots of fish under the water as the lens cuts out reflecting glare in exactly the same way as do polaroid sunglasses for the eyes. Also, when the sun is very bright and the light intense, a polaroid filter has the advantage of deepening the colour that can otherwise look a bit hazy and washed out.

I also like a sunny cross lens – the type that just gives a little bit of star burst on the fish when you are holding it in sunlight. This is not a feature to overuse, but occasionally it can look rather pretty and also highlight the beauty of the fish.

That is probably the keynote with the use of all filters: do not overuse them. You can get many filters that will accentuate all colours but I believe it is best to record the real thing as much as possible. Nature herself is very hard to better.

Pressure-Release Cables

Most cameras have a shutter-delay action. You set the camera, press the shutter and in ten to thirty seconds you hear the click of the photograph being taken. This is perfect for family groups, but useless for fishermen. Five to six shots, which is the minimum you will need of a good fish, would take three to five minutes! A pressure-release cable closes the shutter for you, and providing the film rewinds automatically or you have a winder or motor drive on the camera, you can shoot an entire film in thirty seconds! This facility is essential for the man who fishes alone. You will also need a tripod if you are taking your own shots. There are attachments for simple rodrests. You screw the camera on your rod-rest and this cuts down carrying weight. The problem is that in a breeze the camera is very unstable and blurred shots are inevitable. A good, strong, stable tripod is a far better bet, even if it does add on those extra few pounds of luggage. As with everything, you tend to get what you pay for, and the more money you spend on your tripod the more features it will offer and the more robust it is likely to be. Choose one very carefully but make sure its legs offer a good range and it is stable enough to support the weight of your camera and perhaps a long lens.

Flashguns

Don't skimp on your flashgun. Make sure you buy one powerful enough for the job, and make sure it is fully integrated to the camera you are using. Also carry a torch when you are going to use the flashgun. You can set your focusing in the torch beam or in front of the car headlamps if you are close enough. Remember, even auto-focus cameras can struggle in pitch darkness.

Films

The decision you have got to make is whether to go for print, transparency or black and white. Sadly, the latter seems to be on the way out these days, which is a shame. I, personally, feel that some of the moodiest, most atmospheric photographs of angling ever taken were in the black-and-white format, but now we seem to live in a colour-crazy world. If you are still interested in black and white films, then a speed of 400 ASA is about right for most conditions.

Colour print films are quick, cheap and generally quite efficient. At the end of your session, or holiday or whatever, you have a handful of nice prints to show everybody. However, you must realize that prints are rarely of a high enough standard for reproduction in good-quality magazines or books. If you aspire to these things, then colour transparency film is essential. Speed of film is all important. As a rough guide, if the light is very good then a 50 or a 64 ASA film will enhance the colours very strongly. If the light is not quite this brilliant then a 100 or a 200 ASA film will be quite adequate. For those rather gloomy autumn or winter days, a 400 ASA film is probably what you need.

Most makes are very good these days, and over the years I have had excellent results with Ektachrome. These days, however, I mostly use either Fuji or Agfa. Both of these offer process-paid films. My current favourite is Agfa, and the speed of their service is unrivalled. I find their greens absolutely perfect – an important consideration for the angler.

Finally, always remember to buy a good, strong, rugged, waterproof case to carry your cameras. They take a great deal of battering in often very unpleasant conditions. They are valuable, so take care of them. And finally, always remember to have spare batteries for camera, motor drive and flashgun. There is nothing worse than catching the fish of your dreams at ten o'clock on a winter's night on Sunday and finding the flash batteries have expired.

18 Tackle Tips

In no particular order, here come a welter of tackle tips prompted by many friends and fishing partners of the past and the present. Thanks to all!

Towels, which are so useful for the swimfeeder fisherman in particular, can be bought very cheaply at car boot sales.

If a fish becomes weeded, try hand-lining. Point the rod straight at the problem area, hold the line tightly between the fingers and pull in a sawing motion. This will exert far more pressure than the rod can put on and could get the fish moving. If this does not work, let the line go slack for up to five minutes and you might find that the fish swims out of the weed or the tree roots of its own accord.

If you put your sharp-ended rodrest straight into a holdall, the points can in time wear a hole in the fabric. It is not a bad idea to line the rodrest compartment with part of a plastic bottle, some cardboard or anything that protects the expensive body of the holdall.

If you have no power gum, try a thin elastic band for making a stop knot.

Buckets are an essential item for most anglers and they can be bought far more cheaply at builders' merchants yards than in ordinary hardware shops.

If you do a lot of night fishing, it is a good idea to make sure that your torches emit red rather than white light. This can be done by using a red bulb or by colouring the torch face with a red marker pen. Red light is less likely to scare fish and is kinder on the eyes. Also, wildlife is generally unafraid of a red light and you might see some interesting things after darkness.

Most shop-bought float boxes are simply rigid plastic affairs. It pays to glue some foam rubber into the top and bottom lid sections so that the floats do not chip as they are being carried, and slide up and down.

Is a friend or relation going to America? Send for some catalogues and mark out the spinners, plugs or other fishing equipment that you want. You will find that it is far, far cheaper over there.

Paint at least some of your quiver-tips white with a bottle of liquid paper. These will show up much better at dusk, dawn and at night in a torch beam.

Never leave old bread, cheese or bait in any net or fishing jacket pocket – certainly not in an outside hut. Mice – and even worse, rats – will scent it out and bite their way through whatever stops them from getting at an unexpected food source.

If at all possible, try and buy the large catering cans of sweetcorn. These weigh over 4lb and work out much more economical than the 11oz tins.

If the wind or the drag it sets up proves too much for a swing-tip it is better to put on a longer one than weigh down the one you have with lead.

When putting swan-shot on the line – for example, when night legering for chub – a good idea is to thread it on a piece of half-metre silicon tubing first. This acts as a cushion with the shot pinched over it in the required place. This precaution is particularly important with the modern copolymer lines, are not very resilient to damage. Another good thing about this is that the shot tends to fly off more easily if they are snagged.

Look up before you tackle up! We all know carbon fibre is a great conductor of electricity so never fish within thirty-five yards of an electric cable. Remember that your rod does not actually have to touch the wires, as electricity can leap the gap.

Try to keep your reels in pouches, or put elastic bands over the spools in your tackle bag. Nothing is worse than a massive jumble of line that seems to trap every piece of tackle.

When considering sleeping bags, buy the warmest one you can find – providing it has a zip opening. You can always unzip it and spread it over you like a duvet if you are too hot to sleep inside it.

Polaroid glasses, I have found, are best with light brown lenses rather than dark blue ones. They seem to let more light into the water on overcast days.

If you have a multiplier, be very careful not to let it fall on sand or grit as a single piece can destroy the smooth running of the reel. Remember when casting to use a progressive pendulum-type movement.

If you are re-waxing your fishing jacket you can get the wax into the seams if you melt it with a hair-dryer. Put the hair-dryer within two inches of the seam and you will find the wax simply streams into these most vulnerable areas.

When out trolling on a big water, if possible set out fishing upwind. It is just possible your engine might fail, and it is far easier to row back with the wind in your favour.

The PVA bags from Gardener Tackle are excellent for putting out particle baits around the hook. Put the bomb, the hookbait and the free particles into the bag, dampen it with a cloth and mould it on to the line. The bag will dissolve on the bottom and allow the hookbait to lie amongst the particles in the most natural way.

Don't forget a target board placed behind a quiver-tip helps to show up the tiniest of bites – often from quite big fish.

When using a closed-face reel for close-in stick work, putting just a small amount of line on the spool will prevent the line bedding in to the layers beneath. Fifteen to twenty yards of line will be enough for most situations.

If you are fishing at night, casting in the dark can be quite difficult. Try to mark out the silhouette of a tree on the bank opposite so that you always have something to line yourself up with. Also, it pays to cast in the daytime to get the length right. When the bait is out the required distance, tie 1–2in of nylon on to the main line. At night you will hear this go through the rings and you can feather the bait down to the exact position you want.

When tying spade-end hooks by hand or machine smear on a coating of superglue or fast-drying varnish afterwards to make quite sure of the knot.

A cheap, beach-style windbreak pegged around the open sides of your umbrella makes a very economical, albeit temporary, bivvy.

After use, dry your rod on a soft cloth for the damp will lift the epoxy coating and destabilize the rings. In the same way, do not store rods in damp bags or sealed rod tubes. Do not grease the ferrule of your rod. This will merely attract dirt and particles of grit will stick and cause wear and tear.

If, on a very cold morning, the line is freezing on your rodrings, give them a coat of glycerine which can be bought from any chemist. This will stop the problem.

A perfect deadbait float can be made from a 1¼in polyball. Simply push in a short piece of stiff rig tube and glue it in place. Glue in a swivel to the open end of the rig tube as a bottom eye for the float. This will be attached to the main line by a small link swivel. This type of float has many advantages. You can take many different coloured polyballs and easily replace one for the other so you always have top visibility. For example, if you are fishing into light water, simply clip on a black float, or, if the sun is behind, you then move back to a white polyball. Casting is also easier with the polyball deadbait float. Any float invariably comes up the line when casting, hits the stop knot and takes the power out of the cast. Because a polyball is so light this does not matter nearly so much.

When travelling, trolling or fishing in heavy rain it is a good idea to keep all your cameras in proper Tupperware boxes – not cheap imitations. You fit a couple of bodies, a couple of lenses and some spare rolls of film and pad them with tissue paper. That way, you know they will be perfectly safe even if dropped into the river!

Black bombs and black hookrigs are all right and are generally used, but in highly fished waters the carp will see these as mechanical, straight shapes and be wary. If you mottle the bomb and the end line with brown enamel paint, the shape will be broken up and the carp will be put off guard.

Don't forget to tie your sunglasses on to a length of cord so that you don't drop them in the river if they slip off your nose when you are climbing trees.

If you keep your hooks in small boxes, smear these with petroleum jelly. This stops the hooks from rusting. It also stops them moving about and blunting their points. The petroleum jelly is odourless so it does not deter fish in any way.

If you are using spade-end hooks – tied either by machine or hand – put on a layer of superglue or fast-drying varnish afterwards. This increases the safety margin and is very useful, especially for feeder fishing when hefty specimens can be expected.

Change your line two or three times a year if you do any amount of fishing. Despite the UV stabilizer now put into most lines, they do deteriorate in sunlight.

If a stick float rises in the water when you are holding it back, there is probably not enough shot on the line. Shot a stick float until it just sinks and then remove a size six and the balance should be perfect.

In cold weather, enlarge the holes of a swimfeeder with scissors or a shop-bought hole enlarger to allow sluggish maggots to escape faster.

In the winter, baits like meat and cheese can be softened by kneading them up with cornflour. The aim is to make them just tough enough to stay on the hook but succulent enough to tempt a very cautious fish.

When fishing shallow, clear water on a sunny day, try blackening the last few yards of line with a waterproof black marker pen. This dulls the glint of the nylon and can result in many more bites.

When legering, it can pay to tug the line between reel and bottom ring occasionally. A bait that moves from time to time can trigger an instant bite.

When float fishing, always take a black waterproof marker pen with you. If the swim has a highly reflective surface just tipping the float top back makes it instantly highly visible.

When fishing shallow water – on the lead especially – soak the *entire* spool of line in luke-warm, soapy water overnight. A number 8 shot eighteen inches above the float allows for better control in a strong up or downstream wind.

Before groundbaiting in a stillwater, throw in a little floating bread to check the amount of drift. In just a light wind, enough current can be generated to carry wrongly positioned groundbait right out of the swim.

Think very carefully before putting unnecessary legerstops or swivels on the line. These are bound to present potentially weak points and do not necessarily do any good at all. Don't follow a trend clone-like, but think your method out for yourself.

Smear your plummet or bomb with petroleum jelly or grease. This will pick up particles off the bed and help you realize if you are fishing over clear sand or gravel.

When you are catapulting groundbait out, go for a low flight path in a wind as it is less likely to be blown off-course.

A shock-leader (a length of 15–20lb line tied to the main reel line) serves two purposes. Firstly, if you are trying to achieve maximum distance, it bears the force of the cast that would otherwise break a lighter line. Secondly, it is more abrasion resistant than 8–10lb line and better able to stand chafing on gravel bars. Sylcast 15lb or 18lb line is a favourite brand and most people use 25–35ft.

WD40 is perfect for getting a reel to run smoothly again. Spray the reel and allow half an hour or so for the oil to penetrate. Then wipe off the surplus.

It is a good idea to put some maggots in an ⅛in of water for half an hour with the lid on the box. You will find they absorb the water and float. This means that the hook weight is neutralized, and is that much more easily sucked into the mouth of a feeding fish.

19 The Last Cast

I am sitting here at the moment on the last day of the fishing season 1992–93. The weather is excellent for the time of the year and the lake in front of me is quite small, deep and clear. There are some super perch here. The point of my telling you this is that the rods that I am using are virtually antique: they are around 11½ft long in hollow glass with a test curve of around 1¼lb. We used to call them Tench Tamers, and I last used mine in around 1976 for long-range tench fishing on the swimfeeder. They had lain retired in my shed for nigh on twenty years, until I suddenly realized that they would be ideal for the job now in hand – that is livebaiting with very small roach for these big perch. So far today, I have landed two good perch and lost a third – through no fault of the rods. As I expected, these ancient Tench Tamers have been perfect. The moral is that gear might go out of fashion, seem to be superseded and be no longer trendy, but it can still be quite serviceable and do a job more than adequately.

I used to fish with an ex-pupil of mine in the days when I was a schoolteacher: it seemed that his whole joy was not so much fishing but collecting tackle. We would sit at the river bank: I would be intent on my fishing while he constantly trotted up to me to show me his latest purchase. Graham did not catch many fish with all this superb tackle – in fact he hardly fished at all, so busy was he buying it, showing it off, polishing it and generally looking after it. I suppose that he was happy in his own way but again there is a lesson here: do not let tackle mania take over; keep your interest in tackle in its proper place and in perspective.

Nice tackle is a joy to use and can make difficult jobs appear easy, but even the very best of tackle is not everything. I often think our grandfathers and great-grandfathers caught fish despite their tackle not because of it, and they probably knew that watercraft and knowledge of fish was much more important than the latest fad or design. All the great tackle in the world will not make a great angler, and a truly good angler, can catch fish on a broom-handle.

Inevitably, a lot of this book will be out of date, in some ways, by the turn of the century. Tackle is big business these days, and the huge companies can afford to spend a fortune testing new materials and ideas. There is a constant striving to get ahead of the field and to beat the competition, and this shows no sign of decreasing. In short, it looks as though tackle ideas will continue to develop in leaps and bound for the foreseeable future. However, hopefully, this book will teach you what to look for when making your choices, and how to avoid a great deal of the hype and advertising rubbish that goes with modern developments. The important thing to remember is always to think for yourself and to stick with basic rules. Make sure that the

THE LAST CAST

The sun creeps up on a new scene.

tackle you are thinking of buying and using fits your particular situation as well as possible. It is your sport, your tackle and your money: do not be brainwashed by anybody.

I wonder where you keep your tackle. When I was a child, my father built me a hut at the bottom of the garden, probably to get all the disgusting, smelly stuff out of the washhouse. I used to love going down there, especially in the close season on a warm Sunday afternoon. The place smelt beautifully of past successes: nets once wet and slimy never really dry out again but are always permeated with the faint aroma of scales and slime. Then there was the smell and sight of rods recently varnished and the comforting odour of waxed waterproofs. Today, tackle sheds also reek of the thousand and one new bait additives, whose smells remain pungent. By about April or May, if I remember, the first of the huge bluebottles would begin to appear – hatched from maggots which escaped steadily throughout the winter. Some afternoons just killing the things or letting them go would be almost a full-time job. I am not so lucky nowadays and my tackle shed is an old outside toilet on the end of my house. It has no window, is flaking and decrepit and seems as though I can never really get it clean or wholesome. Still, I enjoy being in there just messing about with floats, hooks, lures or whatever – pretending that I am busy and that somehow I will be improving my chances in the forthcoming season.

Like me, you probably find that your tackle shed is a kind of island retreat from whatever worries are harassing you at the time. On those long-ago Sunday afternoons, my tackle shed provided an escape from homework; today the outside toilet offers a little peace away from bills, tax demands and urgent letters. Putting new line on spools or re-whipping new rodrings might not be as good as fishing itself but as far as I am concerned, it beats virtually every other human activity out of sight. It seems that if you can't be fishing there is nothing, simply nothing, like messing about with tackle.

Index

INDEX